Lockheed Blackbirds

**A YF-12A flashes its XAIM-47 bay and IR 'eyes'
on a press day in 1965.** *Lockheed*

Lockheed Blackbirds

Anthony M. Thornborough & Peter E. Davies

IAN ALLAN LTD

First published 1988

ISBN 0 7110 1794 8

© A. Thornborough and P. Davies 1988

Published by Ian Allan Ltd, Shepperton, Surrey;
and printed by Ian Allan Printing Ltd at their
works at Coombelands in Runnymede, England

All drawings by M. Keep

Sole distributors for the USA

Publishers & Wholesalers Inc
Osceola, Wisconsin 54020, USA ®

GLOSSARY

AINS	Astro-Inertial Navigation System (SR-71)
AWACS	Airborne Warning & Control System
Blackbird	Popular name for the SR-71, though more correctly the generic term used to describe all of the ADP's (Skunk Works) secret surveillance aircraft. 'Black' is a euphemism for 'secret'
BW	Bomb Wing
CIA	Central Intelligence Agency
C^3/I	Command, Control, Communications & Intelligence
DACT	Dissimilar Air Combat Training
DAFICS	Digital Automatic Flight Inlet Control System
DIA	Defense Intelligence Agency
ECM	Electronic Counter-Measures
EGT	Exhaust Gas Temperature
EOB	Electronic Order of Battle
DARPA	Defense Advanced Research Projects Agency
Dragon Lady	USAF nickname for the U-2/TR-1
FEBA	Forward Edge of the Battle Area
FL	Flight Level (given in hundreds of feet)
FLIR	Forward-Looking Infra-Red
Glossies	Photos and other 'hard-copy' products of reconnaissance
Habu	USAF nickname for the SR-71
HASP	High Altitude Sampling Program
JCS	Joint Chiefs of Staff
MIA	Missing in Action
PSD	Physiological Support Division
QRA	Quick Reaction Alert
Pave Tack	FLIR attack sensor used by the F-111F
RPV	Remotely-Piloted (unmanned) Vehicle
SAS	Stability Augmentation System
SRS/W	Strategic Reconnaissance Squadron/Wing
TACAN	Tactical Air Navigation
TEB	Tri Ethyl Borane
TRAM	FLIR attack sensor used by the A-6E

Front cover:
SR-71A 64-17974 parked on the ramp at March AFB, California in November 1981. *Frank B. Mormillo*

Back cover, top:
Bearing its Det 1 tail marking coiled in a little white Habu, SR-71A 64-17975 makes for the runway at Kadena, Okinawa. *MAP*

Centre:
'Hump-back', twin-seat TR-1B 80-1064 taxies preparatory to a Stan/Eval checkride sorties at Alconbury on 17 March 1987. *Peter R. Foster*

Bottom:
A well-laden TR-1A, 80-1077, carries ASARS-2, Sideways-looking infra-red and intelligence and data-link antennae as it taxies down the runway.
Peter R. Foster

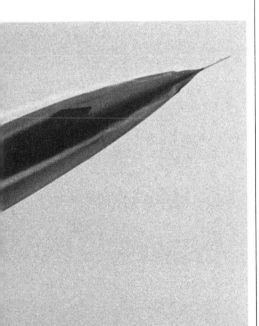

Contents

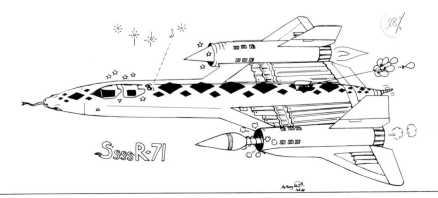

Introduction

One of the longest-standing paradoxes in the public's perception of military aviation is the attitude to reconnaissance aircraft. The world's press may have some grounds for getting excited about formidable destructive devices like the 'F1-11' or Tornado, but the *unarmed* U-2 and SR-71 have always commanded much greater footage of violent prose. The U-2, in particular, has always given offence and this has remained strong for nearly 30 years since the wreckage of Francis Gary Powers' fragile machine fluttered down to Soviet soil in 1960. This event, and subsequent visits to Europe by U-2s in 1962, were powerful ammunition to the growing anti-nuclear lobby. As late as 1979, the solitary U-2R at RAF Mildenhall was despatched to a locked hangar for the base's Open Day on the specific orders of the Ministry of Defence, while in 1975 the five U-2Cs which visited the UK were painted prettily in shades of grey: the normal high-altitude black finish was thought to be far too inflammatory because of its Blackbird associations with the aircraft's CIA spyplane past. When the TR-1 was introduced to the USAFE's theatre the new designation of an aircraft which closely resembles the U-2R was quite deliberate. The Air Force was tired of coping with the U-2's spyplane stigma, whatever the role of the new variant.

Similar attitudes prevail throughout the world, with complaints about overflights playing a leading role in a dozen propaganda wars and several real ones. The persistent furore is, of course, a tribute to the unparalleled importance of a family of aircraft which originated in the early days of the Cold War under the guidance of one man — Clarence L. 'Kelly' Johnson of the Lockheed aircraft company. His

Blackbirds are as busy as ever in the age of satellites and C³I, and there is no sign that they will be made redundant in this century, at least.

But many people ask: 'Why have "spyplanes" when satellite technology is available, and in such widespread use?' The answer is relatively straightforward: satellites are not always up to the job at hand. The same line of reasoning that decreed that the surface-to-air missile (SAM) would render all tactical aircraft obsolete spawned the equally fallacious argument that a relatively immobile object in Earth orbit could take over the work of aircraft in the upper skies. Reconnaissance jets are infinitely more flexible: their equipment can be tailored on a mission-to-mission basis by simple down-loading and sensor replacement using modular pallets; they can be called upon to be at the right place at the right time; information gleaned is significantly more difficult to intercept — in fact, impossible, short of downing the aircraft, if the customer is prepared to wait a short time; and the lower altitude sensors of reconnaissance aircraft are often the only means by which the necessary clarity — the resolution — of the subject-matter can be obtained. Moreover, satellites need pushing aloft aboard expensive and invariably one-shot power packs. In the aftermath of the *Challenger* tragedy and unmanned rocket failures these launch vehicles are proving to be unreliable (several 'Big Bird' and KH-11 spy satellites went down with them, leaving a gaping hole in US intelligence resources). If the Department of Defense needs the glossies on the table, pronto, there is only one team which can respond instantly: Strategic Air Command's 9th SRW, located at Blackbirdsville,

Beale, and at discreet forward operating locations.

Perhaps more significant, satellites have never captured the imagination of people (apart from the post-Sputnik fever), unlike Lockheed's glamorous Blackbirds. The stunning looks of the SR-71 Habu remain unrivalled, and the diversity of the TR-1/U-2R Dragon Lady's mission equipment — manifested as a multiplex of peepholes, blisters and

antennae — lend an air of demonic beauty. The full pressure suits worn by the crews add that final touch of space-age appeal. Even the most forward-thinking people like to see a man — or woman, come to that — in charge of technology, at the helm. And although they perform a vital job, who can question that the Lockheed-built masters of the upper skies are not also very impressive public affairs ambassadors for the United States? Mere rumours of Blackbirds appearing at air shows attract the biggest crowds, and if the birds make a touch-and-go you can sense the adrenalin exude from the crowdline.

The difficulties of assembling a book on these exciting but top secret machines is exemplified by the vagueness of official USAF releases. Performance of the Lockheed surveillance aircraft is coined in such imprecise terms as 'more than', 'approximately' or 'above' such and such. Radio silence (for the most part) and strict security all add to the enigma. The authors are therefore indebted to those people who brought them as up-to-date as possible with the latest unclassified information, often amidst fleeting silhouettes and the lingering smell and aftertaste of burnt gasoline vapour.

Special thanks go to aviation photographers Frank B. Mormillo, John Dunnell, Peter R. Foster, Ben Knowles, T. Shia, David Mears, and Eric Schulzinger of Lockheed for providing much of the previously unpublished visual impact of this book. No less important was the great hospitality of public affairs specialist SSgt Steven Scholar and Dragon Lady drivers Majs Steven Randle and Bob Uebelacker at Alconbury, the generosity of Habu flyer Maj Dan House, the vital assistance provided by Lt-Col Joseph Wagovich and 1st Lt June E. Green at the Mags/Books

division of the USAF, and Rich Stadler of Lockheed for giving us access to papers and works by those great engineers Clarence 'Kelly' Johnson and Ben Rich of the Skunk Works, and William H. Brown of Pratt & Whitney (P&W). We would also like to express our sincere gratitude to the American Institute of Aeronautics & Astronautics, *Airman* magazine, *Appeal Democrat*, Lt-Col Robert A. Brus at Mildenhall, Win Godwin, Chip Glisson, Sandra D. Ahearn and Thelma Cummins of P&W, Paulo Vinicius Basto of *Aviacao Internacional*, Simon Edwards, Lois Lovisolo of Grumman, Brian E. Lynch of Loral, John Arvesen, NASA Ames, Tim Perry of P.P.Aeroparts, Carolyn Russell of the BMAC, Capt Joseph B. Saxon and AIC Heather L. Schroeder at Beale, and Fran Slimmer of Hughes. Many thanks also to our editor Andrew Farrow for his continued support, and to Alan Butcher and his production team.

Anthony M. Thornborough
& Peter E. Davies
Bristol, England

Below:
A flock of five Blackbirds at Beale in 1987: three static Habus, including two-seat trainer 64-17956 at centre, are under armed guard; an SR-71A zooms over the field; and a U-2R taxies on to the main runway.
Lockheed photo by Eric Schulzinger

1
Unusual Solutions – the Skunk Works

In many ways the Lockheed Blackbirds are typical of Clarence L. 'Kelly' Johnson's designs. They provided practical answers to considerable problems in a highly cost-effective, pragmatic way and the goods were delivered inside budget and time schedules. His motto 'Be quick, be quiet, be on time' remains part of Lockheed's Skunk Works philosophy to this day. Johnson learned these good business habits early in life. The seventh child of a Swedish immigrant father, he quickly absorbed the lesson that poverty could be overcome through inventiveness and untiring industry. In his case, this meant helping mother deliver laundry, selling wild blueberries, cutting firewood — or demonstrating precocious engineering skill in improving his aunt's cream separator by altering its gear ratio. Tenacity earned him his nickname too: 'Kelly' was awarded to him by schoolmates who thought he deserved a 'good fighting Irish name' after a spirited piece of self-defence during which he broke another boy's leg. At the age of 12, he became enthralled by books like the *Collins Book of Model Aeroplanes* and from that time onwards he saw his life as a preparation for one thing — becoming an aircraft designer.

Johnson supported himself through the University of Michigan, becoming assistant to the Head of Aeronautical Engineering. Fortunately this Department had attracted a group of pioneering teachers (several of them Russian) who emphasised the practical approach to aeronautical problems. For example, Johnson learned from Prof O. W. Boston techniques of machining high-strength metals which were eventually to serve him well in making the titanium and steel components in the 'spyplanes'. He completed his three-year course in two

years, tutoring and researching to raise cash, and living on milk and doughnuts to appease the stomach ulcers which remained with him until late in his career. The research sideline meant using the University's wind tunnel to develop streamlined body shapes for the automobile industry. The Pierce 'Silver Arrow', the first 'totally streamlined car', was one example.

An earlier encounter with a less refined 'arrow' settled Johnson's next step. Although he was later to fly 2,300 hours as a flight test engineer, he was rejected as an Air Corps pilot because of a childhood eye injury caused by a careless 'injun' arrow. Instead, he joined the fledgling Lockheed company in 1933 and promptly redesigned its first product, the Electra passenger plane. Lockheed's chief engineer was somewhat disconcerted at Johnson's verdict on the company's post-bankruptcy project, particularly his opinion that it was inherently unstable. However, the results of wind tunnel tests were accepted and Lockheed agreed to install the twin vertical tails which the new recruit advocated and which became a trademark for many of its later airliners.

The twin vertical tails also appeared on Kelly's first warplane — the Hudson. This was built for a British Air Ministry order and he designed it virtually single-handed in a 72-hour session at a London hotel. Like the Electra and Model 14, from which it was derived, it led to a family of multi-purpose twin-engined types. One Electra spin-off, the Air Corps' XC-35, gave Kelly experience both of high-altitude problems and of secret government projects. Delivered to the US Army in 1937, it was the world's first successful pressurised sub-stratospheric aircraft and it won the Collier Trophy for the year. Work on

the XC-35, and earlier designs for aviator Wiley Post, gave Kelly a lasting interest in the problems of high-altitude flight, oxygen systems and pressure suits. In those early flights the pilot 'sipped' oxygen through a cigarette holder to 'avoid the threat of oxygen poisoning'.

World War 2 drew the Lockheed team into accelerated work on high-speed high-altitude machines and placed increasing demands on Johnson's open-minded approach. The P-38 Lightning was the great exemplar. Johnson recalls, 'it was considered a radically different design — even funny looking, some said. It wasn't to me. There was a reason for everything that went into it, a logical evolution. The shape took care of itself. In design you are forced to develop unusual solutions to unusual problems'. The need to accommodate twin air-cooled engines, their radiators and superchargers, and a lengthy under-carriage, produced the distinctive twin-boomed outline of the first 400mph-plus fighter.

In the P-38 pilots learned to cope with high-speed compressibility at the edge of supersonic flight, where the limitations of the piston-engined design made the aircraft, on its designer's own admission, 'too dangerous to fly'. Another new philosophy was needed. Johnson claims that he put proposals for a pure-jet fighter to the Air Corps as early as 1940, but it took the threat of the German jet fighters to produce any real interest three years later. Typically, Johnson set himself an incredibly tight schedule, promising to produce America's first effective jet fighter inside 180 days. And typically again, the resultant XP-80 first flew 37 days before that deadline.

Just one of the problems in developing an advanced, secret project such as the XP-80 was lack of space in the factory which, then at wartime peak, was rolling out 28 aircraft a day. Johnson poached 23 engineers, led by Art Viereck, and accommodated them in a construction of old Wright engine boxes, roofed with a hired circus tent, next to the company wind tunnel. This make-shift unit to deal with Advanced Design Projects (ADP) became virtually independent of the rest of the company. It was the first Skunk Works. The 'official' legend of this famous nickname's origin bears retelling. The strict security of the ADP operation inevitably aroused the curiosity of other employees. One designer supposedly asked 'What in heck is "Kelly" doing in there?'. Engineer Irv Culver's reply, 'Oh, he's stirring up some kind of brew', was associated with *Li'l Abner*, a comic strip in which Hairless Joe stirred up his own brew in his 'skonk works', using old shoes, skunk and other oddities to distil his 'Dogpatch Kickapoo Joy Juice'. Ben Rich's account attributes the 'Skunk' element to the ADP's situation across the street from an evil-smelling plastics factory, while Culver himself reckons the Skunk Works name started as a joke as a result of wartime secrecy and the need to use codenames for each department in the factory. The Skunk Works label has survived all the subsequent expansions and relocations in the ADP's history, and the skunk motif (awarded an official US Patent ® symbol in 1973) frequently appears on its products today. 'Lulu-Belle' was the nickname of the first XP-80 in January 1944, giving America its first 500mph fighter. Although only four production aircraft reached Europe before the end of World War 2 (for non-combat familiarisation), the design enabled jet tactics of a kind to be developed in time for the Korean conflict six years later. During that conflict Johnson's thinking too was ahead of requirements. A personal tour of the war theatre enabled him to glean from fighter pilots their anxiety to gain even more speed and altitude in battle. Johnson responded with his supersonic F-104, the first Mach 2 fighter.

An even more pressing American requirement in 1953 was for knowledge of the Eastern Bloc's true military capability. High-altitude reconnaissance of the Warsaw Pact countries had actually begun even before Churchill's announcement on 5 March 1946 that an 'Iron Curtain has descended right across the European Continent'. By 1950, regular over-flights by RB-36, RB-45 and other aircraft were taking place, assisted by the gaps in Soviet air defences and the stripped-down RB-36's ability to fly above the MiG-15's ceiling. But the Soviets soon showed that they could retaliate with their rapidly developed fighters and by 1950 there were at least 17 cases of loss or serious damage to US aircraft. However, the onset of the nuclear arms race really focused Western attention on the need for adequate intelligence data — the rapid development of MiG fighters was alarming, but the explosion of Russia's first nuclear device in August 1953 horrified Western scientists. Intelligence-gathering 'on the ground' became increasingly difficult and the only way of discovering whether even more worrying developments were imminent in Soviet missile or aircraft research seemed to be high-altitude photography.

The United States had several other types of reconnaissance aircraft in addition to the photo-ship RB-36 and RB-45. Electronic intelligence (Elint) was gathered by RB-29s and RB-50s, which also carried up to 11 cameras and probed the Eastern coastal areas of China and Russia, while RAF Lincolns fed in data from East German border flights. These were backed up by EC-97Gs, and C-130AIIs/ C-130Es (RC-130s), all posing in their normal transport guise but actually collecting Elint and Communications intelligence (Comint) from bases in Germany and Turkey. The RC-130 was also capable of detailed photo-mapping — a later mission elsewhere showed that Cuba was misplaced by 1,200ft on existing maps! However, these large and relatively slow aircraft could not be risked on deep penetration flights and the jet-powered RB-47 became the real workhorse. From 1947 onwards all strategic intelligence was overseen by the Central Intelligence Agency (CIA), a newly-formed body which had considerable funds and enviable independence. Using the USAF as a front it operated a small 'air force' of seven RB-69A Neptunes in the Far East, bearing USAF insignia and pioneering the use of sideways-looking airborne radar (SLAR) pods. The real strength lay with the RB-47 operation, though. CIA 'muscle' and a general acceptance of the need for knowledge led to the formation of no less than five Strategic Reconnaissance Wings, all operational by late 1955. They eventually used 290 RB-47E/H/K models, preceded by another 90 B-47B conversions of which 35 were RB-47Hs optimised for Elint. Operating unpredictably on a Temporary Duty (TDY) basis from locations throughout the world, these units — and the 55th SRW in particular — developed many of the undercover tactics used throughout the strategic reconnaissance world.

Even this force was short-lived, however. The Soviets rapidly improved their radar defences which put any aircraft flying at 40,000ft severely at risk. By 1957 the RB-47 force was winding down. Once again, new concepts were required and Kelly Johnson was prepared to accept the challenge — even though Lockheed was not initially approached for proposals.

Burbank's first spyplane

MX-2147 was a Design Study Requirement of 27 March 1953, based on the ideas of Maj John Seaberg, the USAF's Assistant Chief of New Developments, Bombardment Branch. Unlike many senior military men, Seaberg was sure that the turbojet engine could be made to function at extreme cruising altitudes (where air density is down to less than 3% of that at sea level) if it was combined with the correct wing configuration. The new requirement, codenamed 'Bald Eagle', called for a single-seater capable of flying at altitudes above 70,000ft where there would be no give-away vapour trails. Range was to be 3,000 miles and a detailed camera fit was specified for both search and target analysis missions. The Air Force felt this relatively small-scale project might suit a company outside its normal roster of large-volume suppliers. Bell and Fairchild were therefore asked to submit proposals alongside Martin, whose RB-57D development was seen as an interim solution. Bell's twin-jet 116ft-span Model 67 was selected for long-term study while 20 RB-57Ds were ordered under the secret 'Black Knight' programme. With its huge 106ft wingspan (40ft more than the original Canberra which spawned it), this aircraft took reconnaissance into the stratosphere. It gave SAC crews experience of the problems of pressure-suited flying, high above potentially hostile territory. Nevertheless, it was very much a stop-gap answer. The immense aerodynamic loads on the wing gave it a short fatigue life and problems manifested themselves well within the original 1,500-hour estimate. Eventually three aircraft suffered main-spar failure and

Above:
Article 341, the first U-2, early in its test programme. The arid surface of Groom Lake is all too evident here. The 'Angel' took off unexpectedly on her first high speed taxi run, at less than 70kt. *Lockheed*

Right:
Kelly Johnson with a U-2B bearing the Palmdale registration N803X. The CIA-black paint added 40lb to the aircraft's weight and was relieved only by walkway markings, white cockpit sunshade and 'rescue' stencilling on the nose. The sugar-scoop fairing on the tailpipe was a response to the threat of heat-seeking missiles confronted during the Cuban crisis. *Lockheed*

Below:
U-2R 68-10339 was one of the busiest of its kind. This aircraft flew with the 100th and 9th SRWs, was the US Navy EP-X test-bed, and was the avionics trials platform for the TR-1 model. It visited the UK in 1978 with Superpods and ASARS-2 nose fitting and flew on TDY with Mildenhall's Det 4 on at least two occasions. *Lockheed*

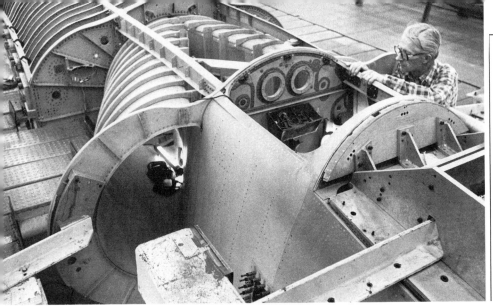

Left:
A TR-1 under assembly. The conventional aluminium structure is common to the TR-1 and U-2R versions, though Lockheed is introducing some composite components and is busy at work with advanced fibre-optic systems and other weight-reducing technologies. *Lockheed*

Below:
A Dragon Lady fuselage being hoisted into position at Palmdale. The aircraft can be disassembled in a similar fashion for transport or airlift carriage. *Lockheed*

one (53-3977) shed an entire wing shortly after landing.

Meanwhile, undeterred by the lack of an invitation, the Skunk Works was tackling the same problem. In 1953 Phil Colman and Gene Frost of the preliminary design department began to adapt the F-104 fuselage to high-altitude flight with a large, high-aspect ratio wing, the J73 engine, and a jettisonable undercarriage. The 'F-104 with wings' submission, called CL282, was passed informally to Seaberg in May 1954, a few weeks after the Bell/Martin decision; but Johnson's considerable reputation ensured attention even at that stage. Initial rejection was based partly on the choice of the J73 turbine: the Air Force (rightly as it turned out) favoured the P&W J57 used in the other submissions. Johnson had been busy behind the scenes elsewhere, though. His design notion had also gone to Trevor Gardner, Assistant Secretary for R&D, several months previously, and it was discussed with senior Washington advisors at length. A totally new initiative began to evolve as the CIA became increasingly interested. Johnson met with its Director, Allen Dulles, and other CIA representatives, including Dr Joe Charyk who supervised the whole high-altitude project. In his extraordinary offer to supply them with 20 suitable aircraft inside eight months for $22 million including spares, Johnson had the support of powerful Air Force voices including Gen Donald Putt, who cited the company's record with the F-80 and F-104. The CIA was impressed — and in a hurry.

Lockheed's CL-282 was therefore re-assessed alongside the Bell and Fairchild paperwork by the USAF/CIA team (now known as the Killian Committee). Johnson was asked to

resubmit, but using the J57 engine equipped with wide-chord compressor blades in place of the untried J73. His CL-282 soon evolved into a totally new aircraft. 'It soon became obvious', he recalls, 'that the only equipment we might retain from the F-104 might be the rudder pedals.' He was left in no doubt that the project was to be pursued in the utmost secrecy. His ADP design team grew to 81 and project 'Aquatone' was directly funded and supervised by the CIA with its man Richard Bissell at the helm. In his estimation, they 'had an almost impossible schedule to meet' after project approval was granted on 9 November 1954. Meanwhile, the Air Force proceeded with its official choice, the Bell Model 67 (now X-16), independently, while simultaneously acting as front organisation for the CIA's Lockheed project U-2, as the CL-282 had been designated. It acted as buyer for equipment such as the specially-modified J57 engines, a small number of which could be easily lost in the huge orders placed for the wide variety of other USAF jets using the type. (When production ended in 1970, P&W had delivered more than 21,000 J57s.) The Skunk Works was well ahead in its designs and began building the first U-2 airframe ('U' for utility, another security ploy), in January 1955. By August, well within Johnson's eight-month deadline, it was ready to fly. Shortly afterwards the Air Force bowed to the inevitable and quietly dropped the X-16. It was all too obvious that the CIA would be taking over the stratosphere in 'Kelly's Angel'.

A less appropriate nickname was the 'Paradise Ranch' title given to the distant dry-lake location of its first flight. Groom Lake was inconveniently distant from Lockheed's Burbank factory but right next to a secret nuclear proving ground — ideal for CIA secrecy. Richard Bissell arranged for President Eisenhower to extend the borders a little, and the CIA then had a private testing area for years to come. Hangars and other structures were contracted on behalf of the 'CLJ Company' (Johnson's initials) and stage-payment cheques arrived in the letterbox at Johnson's home. The U-2 prototype (CIA article 341) arrived by C-124 transports on 24 July and taxi trials began on the 29th. These were carried out with Johnson following the 'Silver Angel' in a 'chase car' (a vehicle which remains part of the U-2 mission to this day), calling for progressive 10kt speed increases. Although test pilot

Tony Le Vier (who had to adopt the pseudonym Anthony Evans for security) was concerned about poor brake response, he took 001 up to 70kt only to find that the incredibly light wing loading made it sail up to about 35ft. Johnson reckoned it was flying easily with the engine on idle — but it did not want to land! Eventually Le Vier managed to stall it back on to the lake bed, blowing both tyres on the single main undercarriage. For the official first flight a more delicate landing technique was evolved. Le Vier allowed the tail wheel to make contact marginally ahead of the maingear in the stall, a procedure used by U-2 pilots ever since. The great event was celebrated with a beer and arm-wrestling party, but the team were on best behaviour a week later on 8 August when the men from Washington came to view and approve the new bird. Testing then proceeded rapidly. With four aircraft in the programme by the end of the year, 70,000ft altitudes became routine. Article 341 eventually crashed out of a flat spin when its pilot Robert Seiker suffered acute anoxia, but there were sufficient airframes to enable the first six CIA pilots to begin training in early 1956. Most were Air Force fighter pilots.

The U-2's designers had no great optimism about its longevity. The light, fragile airframe with its straight 80·1ft wing of 10·6:1 aspect ratio was thought to be good for about three years — just long enough, they reckoned, to stay ahead of Russian interception improvements. In fact, development of the basic U-2 continued for almost 10 years through seven major versions. Many of these were progressive recon-configuration modifications to the original 20 U-2As, although Johnson states that six extra airframes were built 'from spare parts that we didn't need because the U-2 functioned so well'. Later batches brought the total nearer to 53 U-2A/C derivatives, excluding the prototype. Inevitably weights increased as the aircraft's mission capabilities were expanded, and altitude attainment suffered a little. Early J57-powered U-2A models could reach more than 78,000ft with their weight range of 12,000lb (empty) to 22,000lb (gross). The last of this series, the U-2G, sacrificed 3,000ft of altitude for a 2,500lb maximum weight increase. At least five U-2As were converted to U-2B standard, using the far more powerful P&W J75-P-13A or B engine which became the standard power unit for the rest of

the family, offering up to 6,500lb extra thrust compared with the 10,500lb st of the company's uprated J57-P-37. The new engine was very necessary to maintain 'safe' altitudes with ever-larger reconnaissance payloads and its performance was enhanced by specially-developed high-altitude, low-volatility, thermally-stable JP-TS fuel (or LF-1A — Lockheed Lighter Fuel 1, as Kelly dubbed it). The designation U-2C combined the larger intakes of the U-2B with increased fuel capacity and a 'doghouse' dorsal avionics fairing. One composite U-2A/C was remanufactured with a second, raised cockpit in its Q-Bay sensor area and became the first of two U-2CT trainers (56-6692 and -6953 respectively). The five U-2Ds also carried a second occupant in a flush-mounted office in the Q-Bay, and various vertical sensor fittings between the cockpits. About 18 earlier models became U-2Es through improved tail-mounted electronic countermeasures (ECM), and four U-2Cs were temporarily re-christened U-2F while they possessed in-flight refuelling capability. The last confirmed modification included a pair designated U-2G by virtue of their strengthened landing gear and temporary arrester hooks, added for aircraft carrier trials.

There were many other one-off modifications such as the strange U-2C/F 'TRIM', which flew for two years with a massive dorsal canoe incorporating a pair of large 'bug-eye' sensors for assessing exhaust radiation from satellite launch vehicles. Many U-2s bore several designations during long careers. For example, tail number 56-6680 began life as the sixth U-2A, making the first U-2 overflight of Russia in July 1956. It then became a J75-powered U2B, passed to the USAF as a U-2F in 1958 with 56-6707, and served in Vietnam in this capacity with large curved 'ram's horn' electronic support measures (ESM, or Elint) antennae attached to its upper rear fuselage. Restored to U-2C configuration, it subsequently served in Vietnam and Europe, finishing its career with a five-year stretch with the 9th SRW at Beale, California, whence it retired in 1980 to the National Air & Space Museum. Such reconfigurations and rebuilds were typical of the early U-2s, lending considerable credence to the 'Utility' prefix.

———

Despite the adaptability of the airframe, by 1965 Johnson realised that any further 'stretch' in the U-2 would require almost total redesign. After 10 years the U-2's role was still required but many examples had suffered attrition, so the CIA/USAF were happy to place orders for Lockheed's new, 40% enlarged, U-2R (R for revised, though possibly this was originally called WU-2C, U-2N or even U-2L) in August 1966. Higher all-up weights were made possible by a massive 400sq ft increase in wing area, almost doubling it to 1,000sq ft, while span increased from 80ft to 103ft, most of it 'wet', and length from 49·6ft to 62·75ft, enabling a much wider array of sensor equipment to be accommodated and range to be increased. The modular sensor pallet design also ensured that the U-2R would remain as such — there have been no U-2S, U-2T or subsequent rebuilds — although the design later incorporated wing-mounted Superpods of 90cu ft payload capacity, replacing the small 100gal 'slipper' fuel tanks carried by most earlier models for ferry flights. The cramped cockpit of the basic U-2A series was similarly enlarged by 45% to enable pilots to wear a David Clark Co full pressure suit. Above all, the strengthened airframe meant that the extra power of the 17,000lb st J75-P-13B engine could be used without so easily over-stressing the aircraft; earlier U-2s were severely airframe-limited with the J75 installed. At least 12 U-2Rs — and perhaps more than twice that number — were built following the first flight by William M. Park on 28 August 1967. Several aircraft have worn a variety of similar serial numbers as a confusion technique, and the tail numbers game may well be compounded by the fact that both the CIA and USAF received six aircraft each from the initial production lots. Seventeen tails have been 'sighted'.

Development by Johnson, Ben Rich and Fred Cavanaugh of this virtually new airframe, weighing nearly twice that of the early U-2A, enabled the two most recent variants to be added: the ER-2 and TR-1. Strangely, these new models owe their origins to ADP studies into an unmanned U-2R.

In 1970 the USAF inaugurated project 'Compass Cope' with a view towards procuring relatively large numbers of remotely-piloted vehicles to perform high-altitude battle-area Elint, Photint (Photo-intelligence) and Sigint (Signals intelligence) with mission duration in the order of 30 hours at 70,000ft. In the final running were two bids from Boeing and Ryan,

which produced the YOM-94 and -98 prototypes respectively. 'Compass Cope' foundered in July 1977 under budget constraints imposed by the Carter administration, but Lockheed had already been exploring the possibilities of an unmanned U-2R as an alternative solution. The USAF, at the ADP's prompting, began to take a serious look at Burbank's attractive proposals. Experience had taught the Air Force that the U-2R would be a poor candidate for remotely-piloted flight, particularly during approach and recovery (there was nothing big enough to snatch a Dragon Lady in mid-air!), so studies were conducted into reopening the U-2R line with a virtually identical manned model in mind, spurred on by Lockheed's successes with a new range of modular battle-area sensors which were showing promise; perhaps more significant, though less well publicised at the time, the USAF was seriously interested in making up U-2R attrition suffered since 1968. Lockheed grasped the opportunity and went on to modify U-2R 68-10339 as avionics test-bed for the new model, which was received with great enthusiasm. A new mission — dedicated battle-area surveillance — demanded a new designation. Kelly Johnson's account is that JCS Chairman Gen David C. Jones remarked: 'We have to get the U-2 name off that plane. We'll call it the TR-1, tactical reconnaissance one.' Certainly, the whole idea of 'spyplane' overflights had become an embarrassing memory. Negotiations continued in relative secrecy until 16 November 1979, when it was announced that the USAF had awarded Lockheed-California and P&W a joint contract worth $10·2 million to reopen the U-2R line and prepare additional refurbished J75 powerplants, which were becoming available in large numbers as the similarly-powered F-105 Thunderchief finally bowed out of the Air Force. Contracts were signed by Ben Rich and USAF Maj-Gen C. L. Wilson at Dayton, Ohio, after which tooling stored at Norton AFB, California, was taken out of mothballs and reassembled at nearby Palmdale, Air Force Plant 42.

The initial start-up contract was followed by an award for $42·4 million in December 1979, authorised under the Fiscal Year (FY) 1980 budget, to produce two of the new TR-1As and a demilitarised model — the ER-2 — for NASA. The contract envisaged a final production run of 35 aircraft, and 25 were formalised at

this stage, with FY80 prefix serial numbers set aside for future use. To a certain extent the TR-1 represented the first departure from the ADP's Skunk Works philosophy: not only was final assembly centred away from Burbank at Plant 42, but the reintroduction of a programme that had been in cold storage for 12 years meant that new dogs structured around new disciplines had to learn old tricks; Lockheed was grateful to get any of the 'old hands' back, the major challenges being ones of labour management and training as opposed to pushing the boundaries of technology. Lockheed set about its business in a business-like manner. Concessions to the secretive Skunk Works approach were centred around the division of production at Plant 42 into two sites: Site 5 concentrated upon final assembly of the major components trucked in from Burbank, 30 miles away, while the more restricted Site 2 squirrelled the more sensitive avionics into the tubular airframe and slender wings. The first all-new TR-1A, 80-1066, was rolled out of Plant 42 on 15 July 1981, taking to the air for the first time on 1 August with Lockheed test pilot Ken Weir in charge. The first of two twin-seat production derivatives, designated TR-1B, followed suit on 23 February 1983.

Four years later, the status of the production programme is uncertain; USAF public affairs releases state that 24 TR-1A/B aircraft have been ordered, but by late 1987, 25 tails had in fact been noted, excluding NASA's first ER-2, and new ones pop up at regular intervals. Dragon Lady budget requests for the FYs 1980-87 totalled an impressive $1·26 billion, enough for the originally planned 35 machines, and despite certain cutbacks fobbed on the Air Force by Washington the excess should still provide sufficient funds for ongoing aircraft procurement, bringing the total U-2R/TR-1 buy since 1967 up to a *possible* 60 aircraft! Individual aircraft histories on the Lockheed files, unfortunately, remain classified until the year 2011, and the picture is likely to remain obscure until then.

Origins of the Habu
Even if the TR-1 represents the ultimate expression of the U-2 philosophy it will end a much more extensive genealogy than its originator anticipated. Within a year of Article 341's first powered glide, Richard Bissell felt that the team should be working on a successor

Right:
Lockheed's Palmdale facility with a mixture of A-12 and YF-12A aircraft on the ramp. The natural metal example on the right is YF-12A 60-6934. Early examples were delivered in a mix of natural metal and black paint, the black later extended to cover the entire airframe. The date of the photo would be around 1964. *Lockheed*

Below:
Site 2 at Palmdale in 1986. Nine spraylat-coated A-12s can be seen in open storage. Rockwell-Palmdale and some of its B-1B bombers are also in view top right — a later use of stealth technologies.
Lockheed photo by Eric Schulzinger

because the U-2 would soon be vulnerable to interception. On 21 July 1955 President Eisenhower had proposed an 'Open Skies' policy at the Geneva summit, enabling mutual surveillance of military strength by the superpowers. The proposal also prepared the way for the overflights which America intended, whatever the Soviet reaction. In fact Khrushchev's extreme suspicion of the West caused him to reject 'Open Skies' — and withdraw all the previous Soviet nuclear disarmament proposals too.

It was clear that the Soviet Union would do anything to ensure the security of its airspace.

The Skunk Works' response was predictable: more speed, more height and another technological leap. In 1956 the ADP embarked upon Project 'Suntan' which resulted in the proposed CL-400, a Mach 2·5 100,000ft-altitude vehicle powered by two P&W 304 motors fuelled with 30,000gal of liquid hydrogen. Johnson called his 164ft-long design a 'big flying vacuum bottle' which could have

flown even higher than the other Blackbirds. The sheer impracticability of producing and transporting adequate quantities of hydrogen fuel coupled with inadequate range and lack of development potential in a basically cylindrical fuel-tank-plus-cockpit meant that 'Suntan' was chopped after about six months. However, efforts to find a fuel which would burn efficiently in the thin upper atmosphere continued. Lockheed considered coal slurries and boron compounds but eventually

returned to oil-based products. Shell Oil, with Ashland and Monsanto, came up with LF-2A (JP-7) which could operate between −90°F and +650°F. The drive was therefore available for Mach 3+ flight at height but the new design would have to evade SAMs and MiGs, take clear pictures from above 90,000ft, have global range (through aerial refuelling) and possess an insignificant radar cross-section.

'From April 21st 1958, through September 1st 1959', recalls Johnson, 'I made a series of proposals for Mach 3+ reconnaissance aircraft to Richard Bissell.' Lockheed faced competition, but some of the rival proposals were extraordinary. The US Navy suggestion involved hoisting a ramjet-powered inflatable vehicle aloft using a balloon one mile in diameter, while Convair came up with a Mach 4 ramjet-powered device launched from a B-58 and sketched a delta aimed at Mach 6. The Skunk Works undertook a series of equally futuristic, but more realistic, studies, and the twelfth of these (A-12) was given a limited go-ahead on 29 August 1959, with a 12-aircraft order following on 30 January 1960 after mock-up approval. The A-12 was given the deliberately deceptive codename 'Oxcart' but it was far from slow or clumsy. The design target of sustained Mach 3+ cruise speeds was the most demanding that the Lockheed team had ever faced. At the start of the project Johnson offered $50 to anyone who could find any easy problems to solve. He kept his

Still the only photo of the A-12 in flight so far released. The one-man cockpit and narrower nose chines are the most obvious differences from the later versions. This aircraft flew covert CIA missions from Okinawa, Japan during the Vietnam War and failed to return from one of these on 5 June 1968; all further A-12 flights were suspended and the SR-71 took over the task completely. *Lockheed*

Below:
YF-12A 60-6934 at Edwards AFB, California. Note the infra-red sensors in the chines, the camera pods used to monitor GAR-9/AIM-47 missile separation and ignition, and the chunky canopy structure. The forked pitot protruding from the radome is common to all Mach 3+ Blackbirds, providing static and dynamic pressure inputs to the central computers. Aircraft 6934 was later rebuilt as hybrid SR-71C, 64-17981. *Lockheed*

cash. Literally everything on the aircraft had to be invented from scratch, right down to the paint and the manufacturing tools.

In total the original A-12 concept gave rise to four related programmes: the basic A-12 (proof-of-concept but with reconnaissance in mind); the YF-12A (a long-range interceptor for Aerospace Defense Command [ADC]); the SR-71 (the definitive reconnaissance version, proposed to the Air Force in January 1961); and the comparatively petite

D-21, a near-hypersonic drone. All these proposals harboured immense difficulties, the most obvious being the choice of a heat-resistant material. Johnson chose B-120 titanium for much of the structure, having witnessed the problems encountered in making honeycomb access panels out of stainless steel under clinical conditions for the XB-70 bomber. Prolonged 'soaking' at temperatures up to 570°C was expected, ruling out aluminium, so Lockheed fell back on 10 years' experience of working with

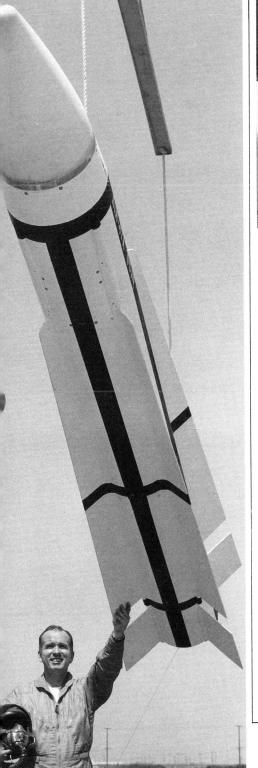

titanium. Test examples of structures such as the nose and wing were built and placed in a 'hot box' to simulate high-speed frictional temperatures. The wing sample 'wrinkled up like an old dish rag', and the solution was to corrugate the wing skins to allow for expansion differentials. These were then mounted on spars using stand-off clips to provide a heat-shield effect and to allow space for distortion. Johnson was accused of building a 'Mach 3 Ford Trimotor' but it was a neat answer, in keeping with the Skunk Works 'KISS' motto (Keep It Simple, Stupid). Titanium is an awkward metal to work. The factory went through two entire manufacturing processes and countless samples before parts of reliable strength and metallic purity could be produced. Some had to be shaped in a massive press operating at temperatures of 1,500°F.

Left:
Hughes test pilot Chris M. Smith face-to-face with the AIM-47 missile, primary armament of the aborted F-12B and forerunner to the AIM-54 Phoenix.
Hughes

Top:
YF-12A 60-6935, now on display at the Air Force Museum at Wright-Patterson AFB, Ohio. This aircraft spent the latter part of its career leased to NASA for a variety of trials including project 'Coldwall', a heat-transfer experiment which involved flying both NASA YF-12s in formation. It is seen here over Edwards with the Air Force Systems Command insignia on its tail.
Frank B. Mormillo

Above:
A close-up of one of YF-12A 60-6935's camera pods. *Frank B. Mormillo*

Other major problems persisted after the bat-like A-12 prototype began its test programme at the 'Ranch' on 26 April 1962, with Lou Schalk at the controls. Its definitive P&W J58 engines were not ready so the first A-12 (60-6924) flew initially with a pair of the proven (but less powerful) J75s instead, limiting speeds to the Mach 1+ regime. Special lubricants and hydraulic fluids had to be developed by Pennsylvania State University, and continuing problems jeopardised the whole show on several occasions. For example, the transducer used to

measure air volume around the large regulating 'spike' body placed in the air intakes took six weeks to sort out. Even the high-temperature-tolerant red and white paint eventually perfected by Ben Rich and used for the US insignia came off after virtually every flight. Where paint was applied over thermoplastic surfaces, interaction with spilled fuel caused it to bubble off. However, the programme made rapid progress in other areas, particularly after the J58 engines were installed in early 1963.

The world's first Mach 3+ cruise aircraft took only 30 months from approval to first flight, driven on by the Skunk Works' inventive energy and the CIA/USAF sponsors' need for a superior machine. A dozen J58-powered A-12s were duly delivered to the CIA, joined later by three more including a J75-powered two-seat trainer-cum-'big wig' visitor-orientation craft (60-6927) in 1962, affectionately known as the 'Titanium Goose'. Covert operations were flown until the aircraft were retired to

storage at Palmdale in June 1968. Its unique shape, described by its designer as resembling a 'snake swallowing three mice when seen head-on', remained secret from the world until 29 February 1964. On that day President Lyndon Johnson officially revealed the A-12's existence, referring to it incorrectly as the A-11 and compounding the confusion by allowing photos of the prototype YF-12A fighter to appear. To be told of a revolutionary new aircraft whose existence was not even suspected

Above:
YF-12A 60-6936 taxying in at Edwards in 1966. Had Defense Secretary McNamara not blocked the money voted by Congress, Lockheed would have built 93 F-12B interceptors.
Frank B. Mormillo

came as a shock to the aviation world and the popular press was reduced to such wild incomprehension that some papers regarded the project as a competitor to Concorde! To be fair, it was associated, in FAA airline briefings, with SST prospects. Further amazement, particularly at Lockheed-California, resulted from the President's announcement four months later of the SR-71 reconnaissance version. Lockheed had assumed that its late 1962 contract was for six 'RS-71', or even 'R-71' airframes, with the emphasis on 'R' for reconnaissance. Although the aircraft was originally envisaged as having a secondary 'S' (strike) role, using a one-megaton pod-mounted weapon, SAC generals saw this as a threat to 'Sacred Cow' B-70 Valkyrie funding and the strike aspect of the specification was dropped very early in the programme. Planned disinformation was probably at the root of all this but it caused a good deal of paperwork at Burbank, where the aircraft was referred to jokingly as 'Strike Recci' for quite a while.

A further deception was practised when the freshly unveiled YF-12A piloted by Col Robert 'Silver Fox' Stephens was allowed to establish a new set of world speed and altitude

Lockheed YF-12A

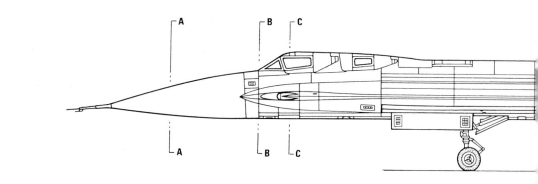

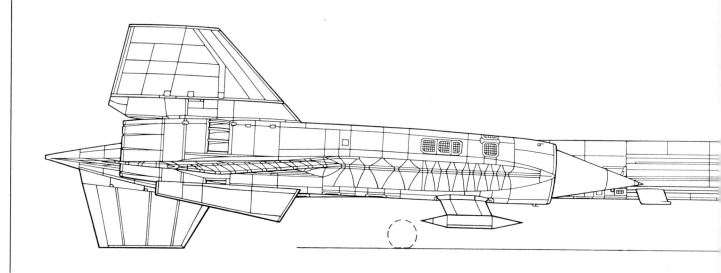

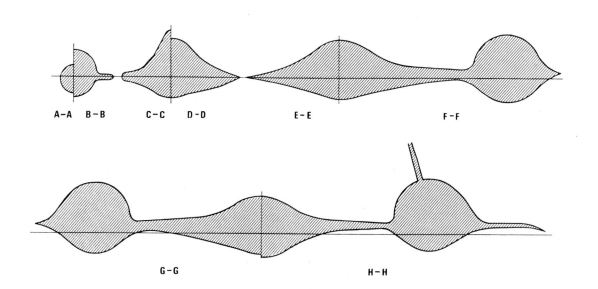

A-A   B-B   C-C   D-D   E-E   F-F

G-G   H-H

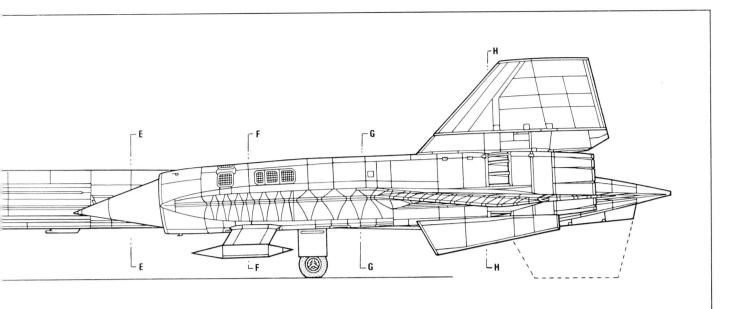

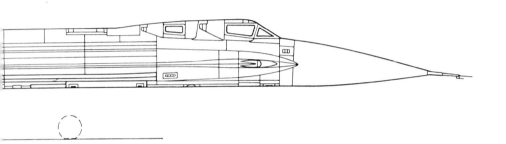

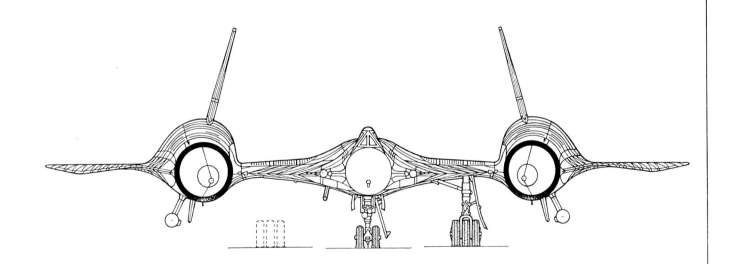

Lockheed YF-12A

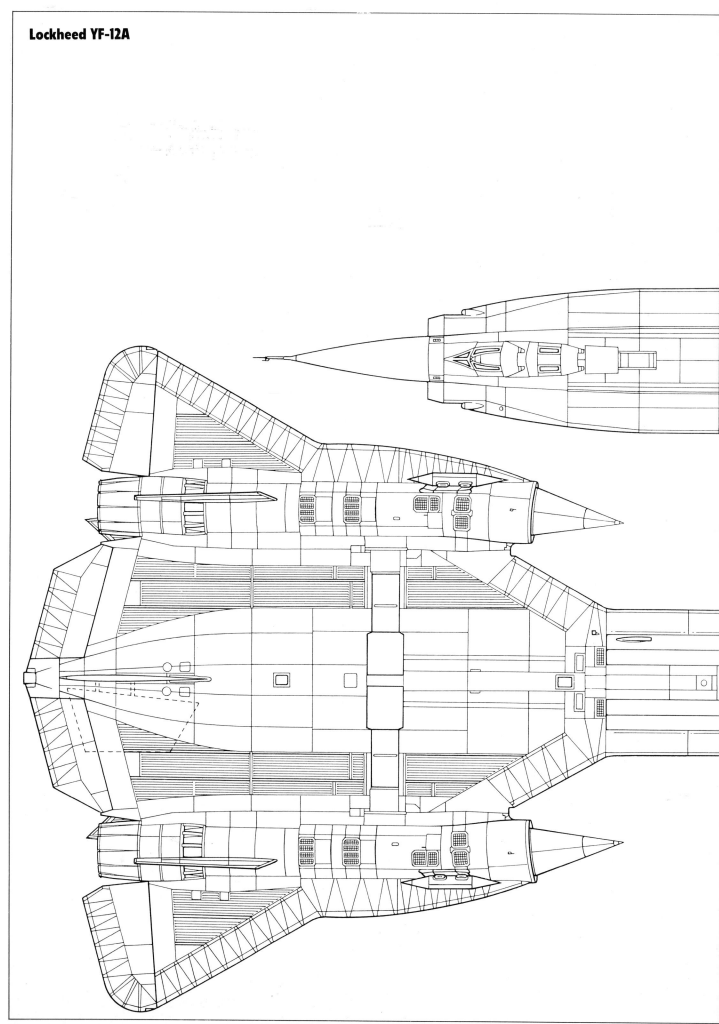

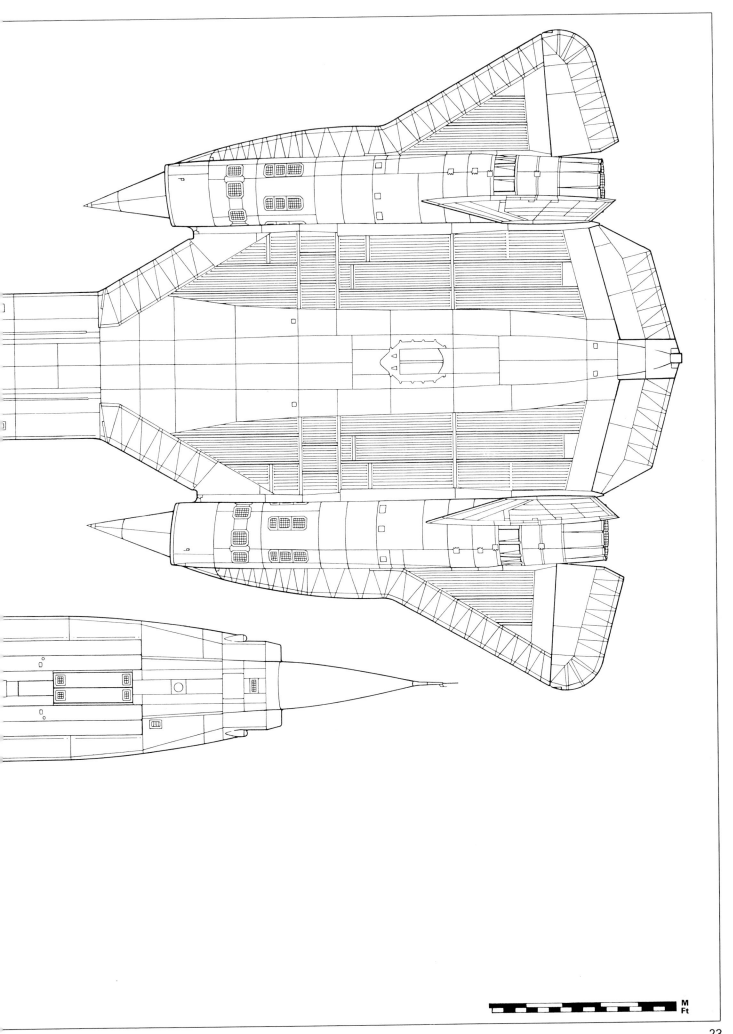

Lockheed A-12

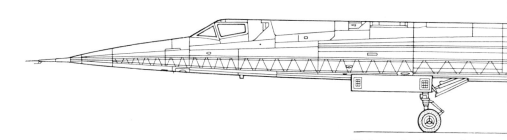

Main production version

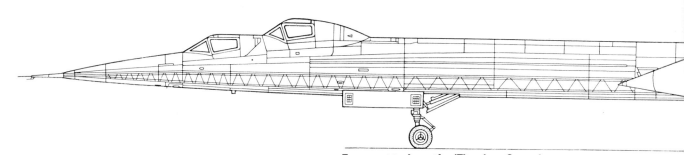

Two-seat trainer, the 'Titanium Goose'

records on 1 May 1965, reaching a sustained 80,258ft and 2,070mph over a 15/25km circuit, among others. In fact, the A-12 would have shown its higher top speed (Mach 3·6) and altitude (92,000ft) if its CIA owners had been willing to divulge such crucial details. Secrecy on the grand scale necessary to disguise the vastly expensive A-12 programme had a dual purpose, of course: secrecy from potential enemies outside the USA, and also from those in Congress who would be anxious to find chances to reduce the defence budget. The CIA method of presenting amounts but not accounts was very helpful in this.

The history of the YF-12 has always been a sore point with the Skunk Works boss. Aircraft 60-6934 was the first to fly, piloted by James D. Eastham on 7 August 1963, the start of a three-aircraft programme that would continue until November 1979. One of the galaxy of myths surrounding the Blackbird programme was that the YF-12 was merely a diversionary cover for the spyplane purpose of the 'Oxcart' programme, rather than a serious contender for ADC's F-106 replacement. Certainly, Defense Secretary McNamara had

announced it as an interceptor and nothing more, but the appearance of the SR-71 so soon afterwards did little to clarify things. Lockheed was offered the development contract for an interceptor variant when cost overruns caused cancellation of the Improved Manned Interceptor (IMI), North American's F-108 Rapier, in 1959. Rapier's Hughes ASG-18 pulse-Doppler radar system and its allied GAR-9 (later AIM-47A) long-range Falcon missiles — which were working successfully — were therefore in search of an alternative carrier. Lockheed's proposal to modify its A-12 for the purpose was welcomed by Air Force R&D people who continued to support the Hughes system in its B-58 test-bed. Lockheed envisaged NORAD airspace being defended by a small fleet of F-12s (instead of the large F-102/106 establishment), meeting supersonic or other intruders around the clock at extreme range and speed. The A-12's large fuselage could accommodate three 820lb GAR-9 missiles (one of the four bays was taken up by avionics) and the sharp chines ahead of the cockpit were trimmed back to provide room for a plastic conical radome for the

ASG-18's 40in dish, and twin-set of conventionally-refrigerated infra-red sensors — the latter being slaved to radar or vice versa for back-up track-while-scan operation against multiple 'bogies'. A retractable ventral fin was fitted to the lower rear fuselage, and two smaller fixed fins bolted rigidly to the engine nacelles, to restore directional stability upset by the nasal alterations. In other respects, the A-12's distinctive rounded delta planform with huge nacelles, canted vertical stabilisers and a flattened fuselage, was preserved. The A-12s were single-seaters but the YF-12s added a second station for a Fire Control Officer (FCO) to acquire and track targets and manage the weapons system. Although the problems of ejecting and firing large, sophisticated missiles — forerunners to today's AIM-54 Phoenix — at unprecedented speed and height took

Right:
The specially configured B-58A, 55-665, which carried the AN/ASG-18 radar and GAR-9 (AIM-47A) missile. The pod beneath the aptly-named *Snoopy 1* houses the missile while the infra-red sensors which later appeared on the YF-12A can be seen above the nose-gear doors. *Hughes Aircraft Co*

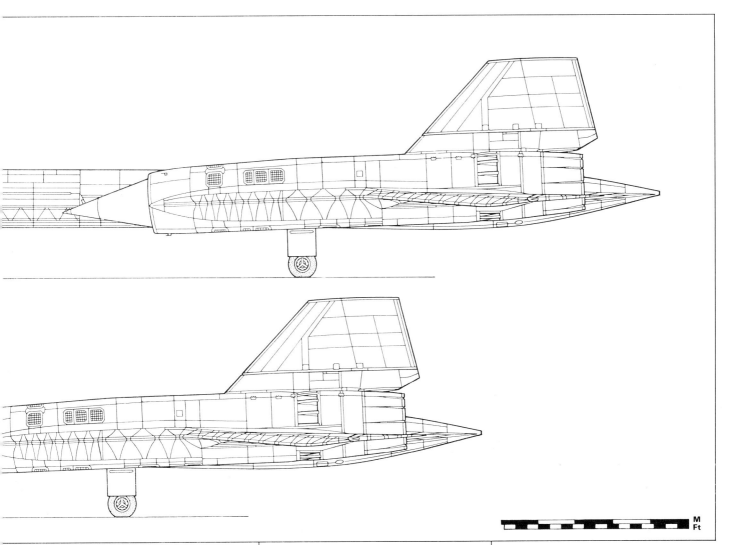

three years to perfect, the results were outstanding. Missiles launched at Mach 3 were able to hit targets up to 140 miles away at altitudes between sea-level and 100,000ft. The missile and sensors combination was soon notching up a 90% hit rate — a truly remarkable feat when one considers that the F-12 *could* be called upon to dash a high-speed target on the nose in a Mach 6 encounter! — and Lockheed felt it had a superior interceptor to offer the Air Force. Obviously it would be no dogfighter but it would be ready to meet any future Soviet threat from supersonic low-level strikers. However, new Secretary of Defense Robert S. McNamara disagreed and saw no need for the F-12 despite the fact that Congress had already voted $90 million towards the construction of 93 definitive F-12B aircraft. In three successive years McNamara refused to free this money, preferring to fund the cheaper 'F-106X', the B-70 (cancelled soon afterwards) and, in due course, his own 'baby' — the F-111. His Department was not content to merely cancel the F-12 project; in true TSR2-style Lockheed was ordered to destroy all the F-12B tooling as well.

Kelly Johnson still feels that the $19 million F-12B would have been ready for the Soviet Tu-26 'Backfire' — the threat which McNamara failed to anticipate — when it appeared in 1974. In his opinion, none of the current USAF 'Teenage' fighters can stay with this low-level supersonic penetrator, or its more lethal successor the 'Blackjack', as effectively.

On CIA orders the three YF-12 prototypes were stored. Half of one of them (60-6934) was used to fabricate 'The Bastard', the two-seat SR-71C trainer (64-17981) which first flew in March 1969, incorporating spare test components for its forward fuselage. The other two aircraft were passed to NASA Dryden, California, in 1969 and gave a decade's worth of valuable service in a variety of programmes associated with sustained supersonic flight, including the American SST project.

Although the third Blackbird, the SR-71, closely resembles its A-12 and F-12 predecessors externally in most respects, the billion dollar programme incorporated numerous improvements and changes, both in capability and in manufacturing techniques. Following the initial six-aircraft contract in 1962, construction of the prototype, 64-17950, began. Internal fuel capacity was increased, instrumentation altered and a new generation of sensor devices accommodated. Gross weight increased to 172,000lb compared with 120,000lb for the A-12, and the fuselage was lengthened from 98·75ft (excluding pitot) to 103·8ft; and broader nose chines appeared. The second cockpit housed a Reconnaissance Systems Operator (RSO).

Considerable improvements were made to the air intake systems, many problems being experienced with intake management on the earlier Blackbirds. The correct balance of airflow over such a huge range of speed and altitude conditions required a long trial-and-error process. Slightly incorrect positioning of the variable 'spike' centrebody in the intake could produce a stall condition

Right:
An awe-inspiring photo of five SR-71s under final assembly at Burbank, snapped during the heyday of Habu production around 1966. Stealth techniques are evident in the zig-zag structure of the wing leading edges (centre) which bounce radar waves out at diffuse angles, the centrebody spikes (near the Lockheed notice 'It's serious. Watch out for Foreign Object Damage'), and rounded surfaces on the rest of the structure. *Lockheed*

in the engine called unstart, where the intake's shockwave was disturbed, causing loss of power and a violent yawing of the aircraft in the direction of the unstarted engine. Lockheed solved the problem eventually and also invested heavily in expensive titanium forging machinery which speeded production of the SR-71s. In one instance a single forged part replaced a component which had previously been assembled from 96 separate parts. The SR-71 is the neatest and the toughest of all the Blackbirds.

Prototype 64-17950 first roared down the runway on 22 December

Left:
SR-71A 64-17964 in a shallow bank. Note the UHF communications antenna protruding out from under the nose area — this retracts when the Habu reaches high speed. *Frank B. Mormillo*

Right:
Robert J. Gilliland, who flew the SR-71 on its 22 December 1964 maiden flight, became SR-71 project pilot after a period as an A-12 tester. *Lockheed*

Far right:
Modellers will enjoy the canopy detail here but the real subject is Bill Weaver, who survived the Mach 3 break-up of SR-71A 64-17952 in 1966 — without using his ADP SR-1 ejection seat! *Lockheed*

1964, flown by Robert J. Gilliland and accompanied by a trio of F-104 Starfighters. The vast experience accrued during the A-12/F-12 phases enabled '950 to be taken to Mach 1·5 and 50,000ft on its first excursion. With two other aircraft soon available the test programme proceeded rapidly and the next three SR-71s operated out of Edwards AFB as the Air Force Flight Test Center took on a major share of development flying. It was and is very much the latter's aircraft, CIA participation having declined rapidly after the early 1960s, though the new bird's induction was not without cost. The old unstart problem, on a grand scale, wrought such severe structural forces on 64-17952 that it came apart at Mach 3 and 80,000ft. Pilot Bill Weaver survived even though his ejection seat never left the aircraft; but RSO Jim Zwayer died in a high-g bail-out. It was the seventh Blackbird lost by 1966. Prototype 64-17950 was also destroyed when the main under-carriage tyres blew out during brake system trials. The resulting fire in the magnesium wheels spread to the whole aircraft as it ran off the Edwards runway. Another aircraft, 64-17954, was demolished in similar circumstances in April 1969, after which new aluminium wheels and stronger tyres with a beefed-up compound were retrofitted to all SR-71s. Thirty-two SR-71s were produced, including two SR-71B trainers and 'The Bastard'. Nearly a quarter of a century on, they are completely unsurpassed as rulers of the upper skies.

Left:
Habu tail number 64-17975 landing at Norton AFB, California. The gear oleos are stretched out but will soon compress when the SR-71 thumps on the runway. *Frank B. Mormillo*

2
Dragon Lady

President Eisenhower was probably well aware that his 'Open Skies' proposals in July 1955 had little chance of acceptance by the Soviet Union. After a barely decent pause following Khrushchev's flat rejection, the well-laid plans for U-2 overflights were authorised by 'Ike' and Foster Dulles in June 1956. The well-established USAF complex in Europe was the obvious springboard. A hangar was designated at RAF Lakenheath and a brace of U-birds arrived by airlift from the 'Ranch'. The ever-wary British public was advised that the so-called First Weather Reconnaissance Squadron (Provisional) — WRSP-1 — would be

involved in scientific investigation of Clear Air Turbulence (CAT), convective clouds, cosmic rays and other meteorological oddities. Unfortunately, no one mentioned where this research was to be done. Even so, a few observers concluded that such phenomena might well occur abundantly over the Soviet Union — and this was indeed where the U-2As were heading.

WRSP-1 moved on to Weisbaden in Germany — closer to the Soviet border and less troubled by anxious onlookers. With some trepidation, the first overflight was authorised for the Fourth of July 1956. It succeeded in everything the CIA had hoped for.

U-2A 56-6680 (Article 347) flew over Moscow, Leningrad and the Baltic coast, bringing back the film to prove it. Four more flights followed quickly, with undercover protests via Russian diplomats providing a useful index of Soviet frustration after the second incursion. CIA pilot Howard Carey became the first casualty, though not to the baffled Soviet defences, when his U-2A broke up near Kaiserlautern on 17 September, drawing unwelcome attention to the 'research' flights. It is likely that he was buzzed by curious RCAF Sabres and stalled out of control. Undaunted, the second phase of the operation went ahead with a fresh batch of CIA aircrew

Below:
A classic view of shiny U-2A 56-6708 with the 4080th SRW before it received its black mantle. Seen here with its citation ribbon on the fin, the U-bird took part in Cuban overflights.
Lockheed

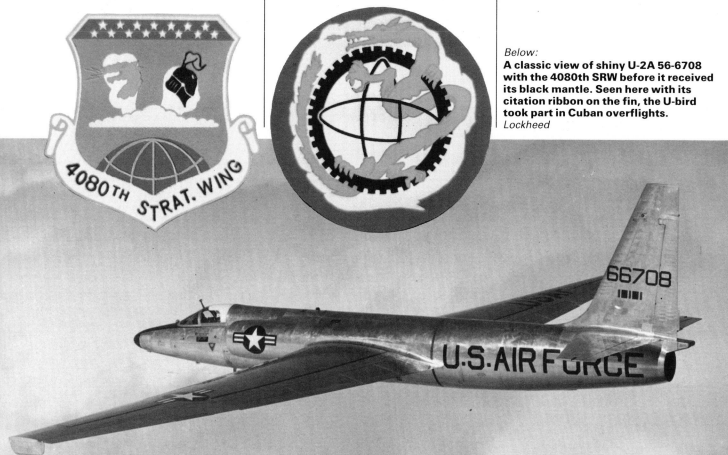

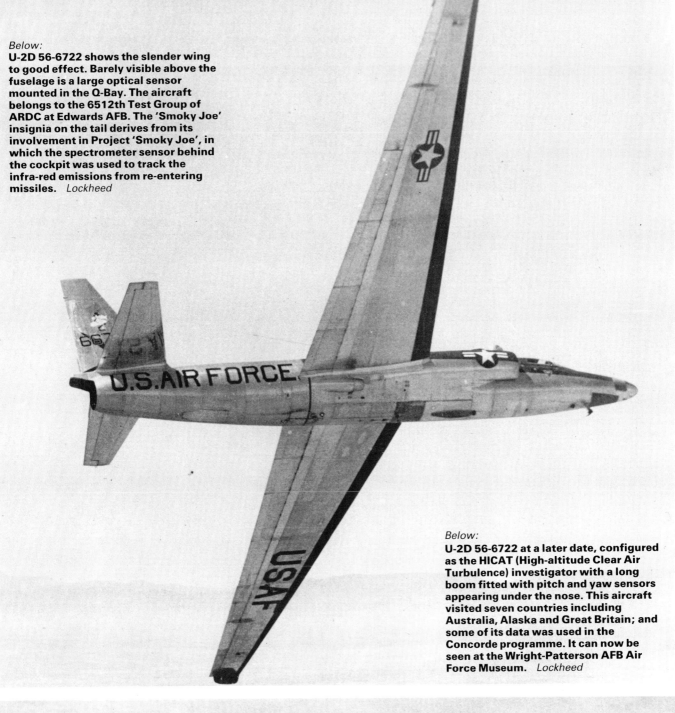

Below:
U-2D 56-6722 shows the slender wing to good effect. Barely visible above the fuselage is a large optical sensor mounted in the Q-Bay. The aircraft belongs to the 6512th Test Group of ARDC at Edwards AFB. The 'Smoky Joe' insignia on the tail derives from its involvement in Project 'Smoky Joe', in which the spectrometer sensor behind the cockpit was used to track the infra-red emissions from re-entering missiles. *Lockheed*

Below:
U-2D 56-6722 at a later date, configured as the HICAT (High-altitude Clear Air Turbulence) investigator with a long boom fitted with pitch and yaw sensors appearing under the nose. This aircraft visited seven countries including Australia, Alaska and Great Britain; and some of its data was used in the Concorde programme. It can now be seen at the Wright-Patterson AFB Air Force Museum. *Lockheed*

taking their birds to Incirlik, Turkey, as WRSP-2, or Det 10-10. In due course they were joined by WRSP-1's crews and Operating Locations (OLs) were established at Peshawar and Lahore, in Pakistan, in late 1957, providing wide-angle coverage of the Soviet bloc. Logistical back-up at this distance was difficult and the U-2s had to return to Van Nuys for major service, bearing fictitious civil registrations during their down-time. As each aircraft was essentially hand-built, spares and panels were not standard.

Despite their apparent invulnerability, the overflights were made with great caution, each one requiring direct Presidential authorisation via Richard Bissell at the CIA. Utilisation slowed after the initial euphoria, particularly as many of the crucial questions were answered by the early missions. The presumed 'bomber gap', for example, evidently wasn't so wide as the CIA had assumed. Soviet progress with the Miya-4 'Bison' and Tu-95 'Bear' was seen to be slower than expected, though ICBM development was moving rapidly. US defence expenditure could therefore be adjusted accordingly, making the U-2 operation extremely cost-effective. The first ICBM, the SS-6, was photographed in 1957 and subsequent overflights were tasked with the job of recording count-down instructions at missile sites together with a basic Elint study of the burgeoning radar network. Sites at Tyuratam, Sverdlovsk, Kasputin Yar and in the Kamchatka Peninsula were photographed, while safer peripheral flights were increasingly made along national borders. The U-2 sensor's 100-mile slant-range allowed a useful watch to be kept. When cloud prevented Photint sorties, Elint and Comint could be garnered instead.

Throughout the late 1950s the CIA's U-2 operation expanded, with a third WRSP established at Atsugi in Japan and further OL at Bødo, Norway, which is still used by Blackbirds today. Secrecy was still preserved with relative success although recurrent accidents drew public attention to the Dragon Lady's mysterious private life. In the USA these were easier to cover up. Robert Everett abandoned his blazing cockpit on 16 February 1956, in the first of four crashes that year. Apart from Howard Carey's, in West Germany, these all occurred in remote areas of the south western USA, Including the training bases at Groom Lake, and Laughlin, Texas. However, the crash-landing of a fuel-starved U-2 from Atsugi on nearby Fujisawa airfield, Tokyo, attracted a good audience in September 1959. Public relations were not enhanced when spectators were chased off by a large contingent of plain-clothes Americans who were instantly helicoptered in. Among other duties, the Atsugi and Bødo flights began the systematic High Altitude Sampling Program (HASP). Atmospheric debris from Russian nuclear tests was carried by the winds and collected by various filters installed in the noses of the U-2s. Analysis of these floating particles may be so precise that they could be identified as originating from the trigger, the case or any other part of a nuclear weapon. The value of this information was so great that HASP flights continued as one of the U-2's primary roles for nearly seven years.

It was the U-2's optical sensors which continued to offer the most spectacular intelligence data. Their capability was first shown in 1955 when the USAF released photographs taken from another aircraft at 50,000ft on which it was possible to identify golf balls on a green. Resolution of this order was possible only because of the parallel developments in aerial cameras at that time. The main U-2 unit, the Hycon Model 73B (the 'B' camera), weighed 400lb and enabled stereo pairs of photos of unprecedented definition in the order of 60 lines per mm to be produced from above 70,000ft. Autofocus and auto-exposure, only recently found in the photographic world at large, were state-of-the-art in 1955. The 'B' camera was the work of Dr Edwin Land and Harvard astronomer Dr James Baker. To take full advantage of its 36in focal length lens, Kodak evolved a new, lightweight Mylar-based film capable of retaining

high acuity images on 18in×18in negatives. Up to 4,000 were taken on a typical mission, giving plenty of work for the photo interpreters who worked directly from the negatives. Other camera packs were available, including the Itek KA-102A 'LOROP', the A-3 and A-4 packs and the RC-10 mapping unit. These interchangeable packs fitted neatly into the U-2's Q-Bay behind the cockpit — not so impressive, perhaps, as the RB-36D's battery of 14 cameras and 22 crew, but far more effective.

Richard Bissell's office knew well that this idyllic situation was but temporary. Russian frustration and veiled protests at being under the lens increased, though obviously not in public for pride's sake. CIA pilots involved in the 30 or so overflights between 1955 and 1959 became increasingly used to watching through their downward viewsights the MiG and Yak fighters or early SA-1 SAMs attempting interception. At around 60,000ft they all stalled and tumbled back, well below the U-2, as their smaller wings and unadapted engines ran out of air, rendering controlled flight impossible. A more tangible threat became apparent when the SA-2 'Guideline' arrived in 1958-59. With the ability to reach the U-2's altitude, better command guidance and a heavier punch, this missile meant very careful mission planning was needed to avoid suspected sites once they were detected. Additional Elint sorties were also scheduled for this purpose. In the thin atmosphere at 70,000ft the lethal radius of an exploding warhead was increased more than tenfold, while the shock-waves of a nearby explosion could easily disturb the U-2's precarious balance. Pilots learned to fly within incredibly small stall margins at these altitudes. At less than 400kt the aircraft would stall, flame-out and lose up to 40,000ft before a relight could be attempted. At 412kt, Mach buffet would begin as the airflow on the wings went supersonic causing stresses which would eventually rip them apart. Flying in this restricted slot required immense concentration and the autopilot would be used as much as possible. Evasion of a missile would be virtually impossible. A moderately tight turn would quickly dip the inner wingtip into the stall speed range, while the other tip would go marginally supersonic. Flame-out and stall would result.

These hazards were well known to CIA pilot Francis Gary Powers as he pulled back on the bomber-type

control yoke of U-2B 56-6693 and let it climb steeply from the runway at Peshawar. He was bound for Bødo, over 3,700 miles and nine hours away. 'Frank' Powers had made 27 flights since joining WRSP-2 with the second batch of Groom Lake trainees. His unit had performed a variety of missions, including surveillance of the British and French fleets and the canal zone during the Suez crisis. Nevertheless, it was still the Soviet ICBM tests which attracted the CIA's interest, and on 1 May 1960 Powers was scheduled to check out the test sites at Sverdlovsk and Plesetsk. Although the areas were known to be defended heavily, the CIA made the assumption that these would be relaxed on the major national holiday. In any case, the flight had been postponed three times because of poor weather. The aircraft, a previous visitor to Lakenheath and possibly the U-2 involved in the Fujisawa incident, had a variety of engine problems. Everything was working well on 1 May though — until a salvo of 14

Top:
U-2D 56-6722 at Edwards AFB in 1965. The white photo-resolution stripes, for an unknown research task, accentuate the bird's gliding stance.
Frank B. Mormillo

Above:
U-2D 56-6954 at Edwards AFB in 1962 with the 6512th Test Group's 'Smoky Joe' fin cartoon. The 'pickle barrel' sensor behind the cockpit had gone but a large communications antenna fairing remains. The aircraft re-emerged later as a black 100th SWR U-2C.
Frank B. Mormillo

SAM-2s exploded around it at 60,000ft. The U-2B collapsed, as did an intercepting MiG-19 below it. Powers was thrown forward by the 'g' forces on his cramped cockpit as the wreck entered a flat, inverted spin. He chose to climb out rather than risk leg injury on the instrument panel in an ejection. He was captured immediately after the long descent.

American analysts were initially doubtful that Russia's missiles could

have reached the U-2, assuming that Powers had been hit at lower altitude while attempting a relight. Kelly Johnson even doubted that the aircraft remains which the Russians produced could be from a U-2, and said so publicly. This provocative tactic gave his security people headaches and Kelly slept with a pistol at his side for several years thereafter in case he was on the KGB hit-list. However, it forced the Kremlin to show its hand. Studying the photographs of the real 'Utility-2' (as Powers' aircraft had been described to him) which the Russians then displayed, Johnson was able to trace its break-up in detail. His conclusions were borne out exactly when he spoke to Powers after the pilot was exchanged for a Russian spy, and Powers ended up with a job at the Skunk Works. Obviously, the Kremlin extracted every iota of propaganda from the show-trial which Powers endured, and rejoiced at the initial American denials of responsibility or knowledge. Before the Kremlin pro-

Top:
U-2D 56-6954 with the 'pickle barrel' in place, projecting behind the front cockpit. *Frank B. Mormillo*

Above:
With slipper tanks projecting from its wings, one of the 100th SRW's U-2Cs returns to Davis-Monthan AFB, Arizona, in June 1976. *Frank B. Mormillo*

duced him as evidence, Powers was said by the CIA to have 'suffered oxygen problems on a weather research flight over Turkey'. This was subsequently modified to the admission that an 'unarmed civilian plane' *had* apparently strayed into foreign airspace. Technically Powers was a civilian, and unarmed apart from his Randall survival knife, but the rest was greeted by extreme scepticism by an anxious world. The bad jokes about CIA standing for 'Caught In the Act' began.

The CIA's response was simply to shut up the U-2 shop. Overflights ceased and all OL deployments were withdrawn. Most of the 25 pilots were re-assigned to other posts. There was a limited revival of activity in the early 1960s when the furore abated but the credibility problem never went away. People who had been told that the U-2 was built to 'collect high-altitude fuel data for F-104 development' would not accept official blandishments so easily again. There was a three-aircraft HASP detachment at

Upper Heyford in 1962, its WU-2As operating out of three U-2-shaped hangars (which are still used occasionally by visiting TR-1s). British links were maintained through joint operations at RAF Watton, probably involving the four RAF pilots who received U-2 training at Laughlin AFB in 1958. Mainly, though, the focus shifted to China where the risks were less but the growth of nuclear capability was just as worrying to the USA. Chinese Nationalist pilots were instructed at Laughlin AFB from 1958, initially on the RB-57D. When fatigue problems ended its brief career, two U-2As were supplied in 1959. Over-

flights of mainland China began in 1960, with the Lop Nor nuclear test site near Sinkiang a major interest. Use of Chinese aircrew distanced the US government politically from the operation, though CIA pilots were flying the missions too. The patriotic Taiwanese, who felt that they were overflying their own land in fact, accepted hazardous trips of up to 4,000 miles — and took the losses too. Col Chen Wai Sheng was first to go down, on 9 September 1962, shot down when he suffered a flame-out. By that time nearly 100 flights had been made, but losses then accelerated, until a dozen pilots and aircraft were missing by 1969. The Communist Chinese never got an intact U-2, though rewards of £133,000 in gold (at 1962 prices) were offered to potential defectors: an F-104 was only worth £100,000. The remains of four U-2s are still on display at Peking's (Beijing's) People's Museum.

Losses were sadly prevalent in training too. The lack of a two-seat

U-2 until 1972 was a major handicap, but the U-2's draconian handling characteristics, particularly in the landing phase, were no help at all. American instructors found their Chinese pupils lacking in everything but courage, with scanty backgrounds in any sort of technology, let alone flying. One pilot, Capt Sheng Shi Hi, baled out of U-2D 56-6955 (a veteran of Cuban overflights) near Boise, Idaho, on 14 August 1964, and returned to crash a second aircraft on 19 December. Whatever the sacrifices, the China operation provided such accurate progress reports on its targets that China's first atomic test could be predicted almost to the hour.

While direct CIA involvement with U-2 receded steadily after the May 1960 setbacks the USAF took an increasingly prominent role in the programme. The Upper Heyford HASP Temporary Duty in 1962 was given official announcement, commanded by Lt-Col Arthur Leatherwood, USAF, and flew three WU-2As in a neat, inoffensive 'Dorsey' grey scheme with full USAF insignia. However, the situation wasn't quite so innocent: the U-2s operating simultaneously at Watton were plain black CIA birds whose mission received no publicity at all. Both detachments were probably monitoring the Russian's 57-megaton nuclear detonation at Novaya Zemlya.

In practice, USAF's SAC entered the U-2 programme under its own name in June 1957, receiving its first U-2As for the 4028th SRS, 4080th SRW at Laughlin, Texas, a year after the first CIA deliveries at the 'Ranch'. Many of the pilots were refugees from the RB-57D flying, adding to the clique ethos of the unit and aiding secrecy. Others were selected from a variety of units via a strict vetting process. One of the first was Robert Powell, with 3½ years on the RF-84F — an achievement in itself! He flew 1,800 hours on the U-2 in 7½ years and went on to become the high-time SR-71 Habu pilot at his retirement in 1974. Cross-recruitment meant USAF U-2 pilots sometimes entered the CIA programme, though this meant they had to go through the third-degree vetting routine all over again! Often they shared the same facilities and aircraft with CIA pilots (or 'Lockheed consultants') in any case. Transfer to other units elsewhere presented a career problem. For their first two years out of the programme ex-U-2 pilots were not allowed to fly over any territory where they might risk capture — Vietnam, for example — on security grounds.

However, it was the CIA crews who got the best aircraft and the juicy

Above:
This two-seat U-2A/D conversion appears to contain a trainee pilot and a rear-seat instructor who is directing his ground-handling techniques. Whether the rod he holds is for guidance or discipline is unclear! This aircraft, with photo-resolution marks on its tail in 1964, is now displayed at March AFB.
Frank B. Mormillo

missions. The 4028th SRS mainly got HASP, hours and hours of it all over the world, droning along at a steady five miles per gallon. USAF-marked U-birds obviously could not overfly sensitive areas so the unit's first five WU-2As were configured for HASP particle collection with no reconnaissance sensors. Meanwhile, the CIA moved on to the higher-powered U-2B and U-2C models and more exciting flying. HASP, known as Operation 'Crow Flight' to the 4080th, lasted initially until 1962 and took the squadron's detachments to OLs in Puerto Rico, Buenos Aires, Alaska, Australia and many other exotic places. Flights of up to eight hours

were routine, sometimes through quite dense nuclear 'clouds', which necessitated a thorough hose-down of returning U-2s.

It was the Cuban crisis which lifted Air Force 'Utility-2' flying out of the HASP groove. The 4080th had always kept an eye on Cuba, but it was a CIA flight on 29 August, 1962 which brought the first proof of Russian ICBM and IRBM sites there. Paradoxically, once proof was obtained, the Kennedy Administration appeared to become nervous about overt use of the U-2; Col Chen Wai Sheng's shoot-down in China and an accidental incursion into Soviet airspace that August had made it wary. Other intelligence reports of the arrival of actual missiles forced the President's hand. The USAF and CIA both began intensive surveillance, with 4080th pilots cleared for the mission after 10 October. Among them were Majs

Randolph Anderson and Steve Heyser, flying from McCoy AFB, Florida. With six or seven overflights a day on its roster the Air Force began to take control of the show, and it was Maj Heyser's flight of 14 October which first revealed missiles actually on the pad. The increasing recon effort drew in the 363rd TRW's RF-101C Voodoos and a big Navy RF-8 Crusader effort, all revealing ever more sinister threats. In all, 82 U-2 flights were launched by 6 December — but not without cost. Cuban-based Mig-21s failed to reach the photo-birds, which had 'sugar scoop' infra-red-suppressive fairings attached to their tails as a safeguard against 'Atoll' missiles. But the SAM-2 found its mark once again. Maj Anderson died instantly when a near-miss sent shrapnel into his cockpit and partial pressure suit, causing immediate decompression.

Three weeks later, on 20 October, Capt Joe Hyde's flight ended fatally in the Gulf of Mexico 180 miles from Cuba — cause unknown. In the most bizarre of the mishaps, 32-year old Capt Robert Hickman took off from Barksdale AFB, Louisiana, flew a southwesterly leg to MacDill AFB and then turned south for Cuba. At some stage things went badly wrong in the cockpit — a suit or oxygen failure probably. His U-2 flew on 3,000 miles to a crash-landing in the Bolivian mountains near La Paz. After the loss of Maj Anderson, crews were wary of overflights and many more offshore courses were flown for continued surveillance after the Russians agreed to remove their missiles and Il-28 bombers. A tacit 'Open Skies' was agreed over Cuba, at least, while the dismantling was observed from aloft and the world breathed again. The 4080th received the Outstanding Unit Award for its part in the affair and its U-birds proudly wore the OUA ribbon on their light grey tailfins, as indeed they had on the occasion of the first award in 1960 — except that the tails were shiny metal at that point.

After Cuba it was back to HASP mainly, with a few more interesting surveillance jobs from some of the OLs and in Europe. Akrotiri in Cyprus became a favourite perch for U-birds: from there they could wheel above the increasingly troublesome Middle East. They also found themselves providing unofficial interception practice for local RAF Lightnings. In the USA, F-101B crews found the Dragon Lady an irresistible temptation for their 'scope wizards' skills

Top:
The ADP's famous Skunk symbol decorates the tail of Edwards Test Force's U-2D 56-6722. At this stage in the machine's career, the mid-1970s, the bird flew with an overall glossy white finish and bright red trim lines. *MAP*

Above:
U-2D 56-6721 at March AFB on display in July 1980. The Air Force Flight Test Center markings were the last it carried in its varied career. *Frank B. Mormillo*

Right:
U-2D No 722's nose was decorated with a list of places visited, including Alaska, England and New Zealand. The Kahuna warning panel protects the aircraft with a very powerful Hawaiian charm. *MAP*

too, but she normally waved off their advances with ease. Even HASP had its moments. Lt-Col Forest Wilson found his U-2 had lost all electrical power on a sortie far from the Alaskan coast. Peering at his standby compass with a pocket flashlight he struggled to NAS Kodiak only to find the place asleep. Wilson pressed on to Elmendorf AFB in an unheated cockpit with his helmet visor steadily icing up and no autopilot to ease the strain of grappling with unpowered flying controls. He made a safe recovery after the 200-mile extra flight, having spent over three hours in the icy U-2. He received the Karen Koliglan Jr Trophy for his efforts.

Extreme cold played a part in the puzzling 1962 escape by Col 'Chuck' Stratton. An autopilot failure caused his aircraft to pitch up violently,

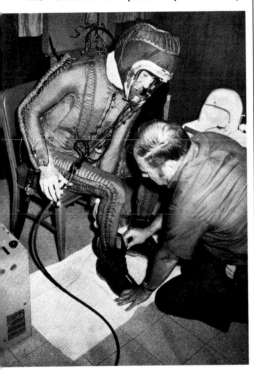

exceeding 'g' limits and breaking off the tail. Further progressive disintegration ensued. Stratton attempted to eject, but his seat may have jammed on the distorted rails. More likely, it bounced back off the cold-hardened plastic of the canopy which had failed to fire off at the start of the sequence. The seat was still strapped in the aircraft's wreckage when it was found, but its occupant ended up on top of a tree in the middle of a swamp, alive and surprisingly well. Rescuers concluded that he must somehow have opened the canopy manually and was then thrown from the spinning, inverted cockpit by 'g' forces. Back in Alaska, the unit was called upon to provide photographic coverage of the effects of the earthquake of 27 March 1964. Three U-2s and a pair of RB-47s added to the pictures taken by a pair of photo-pod-equipped B-58As of the 43rd BW.

The pace of life for the 4080th increased again in late 1963 when President Johnson agreed that a closer eye should be kept on Vietnam. The Wing had handed Laughlin AFB

Left:
A NASA U-2C pilot dresses in the MC-3 partial pressure suit; he has yet to fit his MA-2 helmet, at right. This suit was worn by B-58 crews also. *NASA*

Below:
U-2A 56-6701 carries day-glo panels and non-standard Q-Bay sensors for research out of Edwards AFB in 1962. This U-bird cut its teeth on CIA spy missions, served in Vietnam and later appeared in Europe with the 100th SRW. After a brief service with the 9th SRW it was put on display at the SAC Museum at Offutt AFB, Nebraska.
Frank B. Mormillo

back to Training Command and decamped to Davis-Monthan, Arizona, and by March 1964 all HASP collection gear was stripped out of its aircraft. With optical and Elint packs in the Q-Bays once again, it moved to Bien Hoa, South Vietnam (OL-20). Part of its function was to develop a photo-bank of contingency targets in the North, adding to the work of the first US combat types in the area, the 'Able Mabel' RF-101C Voodoos. This clandestine approach was partly because US rules forbade jet types in the area at this juncture. By April 1965 the U-2 had intensified its activities and detected the first of its old enemy: the SAM-2. Initially these could be avoided, as in Cuba, but they were a palpable threat. The 4080th Wing had its U-2 unit, the 4028th, under the codename 'Lucky Dragon' (later 'Trojan Horse'), while the 4025th Squadron managed the DC-130A Hercules with its Ryan AQM-34 'Lightning Bug' reconnaissance drones on 'Blue Springs' sorties. Heavy losses of other Tac-R (tactical reconnaissance) types to the defences left the RF-4C as the only photo-ship over the North by late 1967, supported by the 4080th SRW in lower threat areas. Under Project 'Ram Rod One' all U-2s were painted in the CIA's favourite colour to reduce visibility in the blue-black upper-atmosphere. They were also fitted with threat warning receivers but their best chance clearly was to stay back from the rapidly growing SAM network and concentrate on Sigint rather than camerawork. The two 'ram's horn' U-2Fs (56-6707 and -6680) were typical of this shift of emphasis as the Photint mission was passed to the expendable drones and the invulnerable SR-71A.

Further changes ensued: on 11 February 1966, the 4080th SRW became the 100th SRW, with 4028th SRS changing designation to 349th SRS. A shift of locale took them from Bien Hoa to steamy U-Tapao (OL-RU) in Thailand. By 1968 over 1,000 missions had been flown at OL-20, but that year also saw the introduction of the far more capable U-2R. Introduced initially into the CIA/Chinese Nationalist programme, the U-2R also appeared at McCoy AFB and eventually in South-East Asia. From then on the U-2's Photint input receded even further as the U-2s became involved in 'Senior Book' flights. To the tactical recon pilots' famous motto 'Alone, Unarmed and . . .' might have been added '. . . bored to death', for many of these flights involved a totally new utilisation of the U-2. In it, the pilot's role was somewhat reduced. 'Senior Book' was a long-term, expanding collection of Comint across the mainland Chinese border. The U-2R driver took his aircraft from U-Tapao, or Osan, South Korea, up to an orbit at operational altitude 'on the border', setting it on autopilot. The various Comint and Sigint sensors aboard were remotely controlled and adjusted, their data passing from the U-2R's real-time transponder through command guidance data-link to a ground or air station. The aircraft would be constantly monitored at ranges of up to 400 miles, or longer if an RC-135 relay was involved; in just over four years of operations the birds flew within a quarter of an hour of assigned time with 98% reliability. Missions of this kind could be extended up to 12hr to cover an area of particular interest and ensure a fair input of data, an adaptation of the U-2's capabilities which is still echoed in today's TR-1 — an electronic 'eyes and ears' in the sky at the automated command of a larger microwave guidance/data system. Despite the monotony of the missions, there was consolation in knowing that their unit was racking up record flight hours — 500 in January 1973 and 600 in December 1974. SAC's Paul T. Cullen Memorial Trophy and the Desportes Trophy for best Reconnaissance Wing in the 15th AF were well earned by the 100th SRW.

'Senior Book', and Laotian overflights for the DIA in search of possible — and highly controversial — MIA (missing in action) POW camps, occupied much of the unit's time until its withdrawal from U-Tapao in April 1976, well after other combat units had left. In the latter stages of the war, 'Olympic Torch' covered its pre- and post-strike reconnaissance work during the 'Linebacker' bombing sorties. The aircraft performed a similar function in 1968 during the bombing pause, in association with the SR-71A Habu. The U-2R's much more manageable flight characteristics gave pilots a safer ride, though two birds were lost; one through a turbine explosion and the other from unexplained total power failure.

Below:
A crisp driftsight view of down-town Seattle, Washington, and nearby SEA-TAC airport, shot in the cockpit of NASA U-2C No 709. *NASA*

The U-2's rather fragile structure does not immediately suggest itself as a candidate for the violent ups and downs of life on an aircraft carrier. Nevertheless, the CIA was attracted to the possibilities of almost unlimited surveillance range offered by a carrier-compatible U-2 as early as 1963. Project 'Seeker' involved a series of bolters by U-2As on USS *Kitty Hawk* to test handling characteristics 'in the groove'. Three aircraft, N-315X, -801X and -808X, were used. A year later, two U-birds (56-6681 and -6682) became U-2Gs for a while when they were fitted with temporary arresting hooks, larger spoilers and more resilient landing gear. Launches and arrested landings were made, the former without catapult assistance. Initially USS *Ranger* served as host but other CIA trial deployments also took place, several of which were operational sorties during the Vietnam War.

With its enhanced performance and superior handling, the U-2R offered the CIA even better maritime prospects. Accordingly, a U-2R with the CIA serial N-812X received the strap-on arresting kit. Between 21 and 23 November 1969 USS *America*

became the base for secret carrier suitability trials off the Virginia Coast. Deck operations went smoothly, with all but wind-over-deck unassisted take-off runs of under 300ft, and landings facilitated by the hook and a pair of spring-steel wingtip skid extensions.

Another U-2R, the long-suffering 68-10339, joined the Navy in late 1972 as test-bed for the EP-X (Electronics Patrol, Experimental) programme. Trials continued well into 1973 with two aircraft equipped with Navy-funded sensors optimised for sea search, including the 'Big Look' AN/ALQ-110 Elint receiver, RCA X-Band radar and a pod-mounted infra-red system on the left wing. Aircraft 68-10339 also had a nose-job, allowing it to carry Texas Instruments' AN/APS-116 forward-looking radar in a more rounded radome for submarine periscope detection (a system which later became standard on Lockheed's subsequent S-3A Viking anti-sub carrier machine). The other main sensors protruded from the Q-Bay and were covered by a large radome under the forward fuselage. Some of the early testing was conducted at Edwards AFB and

one of the modified aircraft flew in natural metal finish before going to sea. The concept of a sea-search U-2 variant was pursued to some extent throughout the 1970s, and Lockheed has continued to promote its big-wing as an AWACS platform ever since, with possible sales to Britain and West Germany a serious possibility at one stage. Background project work on a Condor anti-ship-missile-carrying version has also been explored.

By 1975 few of the original U-2 airframes remained intact. Up to 40 had been lost or seriously damaged in mishaps, most of which could be traced to the specific problems of the aircraft and its demanding nature. Renewed production, via the U-2R line, saved the species from virtual extinction in 1968. Of the surviving U-2A/C models, most remained with the 100th SRW. U-2CT 56-6692, nick-named the 'White Whale', became available in 1973 and was later joined by 56-6953. The training safety record improved considerably from then on. Despite its diminished numbers,

Above:
Two U-2Rs, including 68-10339, were modified in 1973-74 for the US Navy's EP-X carrier trials programme. The rounded radome covers a Texas Instruments AN/APS-116 radar. Wing pods carry a forward-looking infra-red system. *Lockheed*

Left:
An Agency U-2R N812X on USS *America* (CVA-66) in November 1969. Lockheed test pilot Bill Park flew the suitability trials in this aircraft which is fitted with extended wingtip skids (left) and a temporary arresting hook. *Lockheed*

foreign deployments of U-2Cs continued. A pair took up residence in No 4 hangar at RAF Wattisham in 1974, for several weeks. Five of the six surviving U-2Cs, most reconfigured U-2Fs, visited Wethersfield in the UK during 1975 for Pave Onyx trials. Three 349th SRS aircraft at a time flew triangulation patterns to test the Advanced Location Strike System (ALSS) emitter detection system. All were painted in a pleasant, inoffensive two-tone grey — the 'Sabre' scheme — to allay UK government anxieties. All went well until 29 May, when 56-6700 ended up in a German forest only 60 miles west of the East German border. Once again, the press stewed up the 'U-2 Spyplane Scandal', and eye-witness stories that the pilot, Capt Robert Rendelman, was flying from the east when he ejected, all helped to season the familiar recipe. US Embassy officials even felt obliged to explain that a Powers-type situation could not possibly be repeated. In fact, the U-2C had crashed due to violent pitch-down caused by an autopilot failure. It bore many similarities to the accident sustained by the Pave Onyx unit's commander, Col Stratton, 13 years previously. U-2C 56-6700 went to Wiesbaden AB's fire dump and the 100th SRW's last available U-2C, 56-6716, arrived in early June to replace it. Pave Onyx ended in August 1975 and the U-2s returned to Davis-Monthan, and eventual retirement in 1981.

One of the batch, 56-6714, suffered severe nose damage in 1980 when it clipped power lines at Oroville, California, and bellied-in on a muddy field. Capt Edward Beaumont escaped intact — by ejecting after the U-2C had slid to a halt. The Beale Heritage Committee had the U-bird patched up and put on display at Beale AFB, where the U-2s made their final move in spring 1976. The slender machine — returned to its black paint job of course — is a memorial to some very brave men and their unique mission.

Right:
U-2R 68-10337 over Davis-Monthan AFB in June 1976. Once the wheels have met the runway the pilot concentrates on keeping the tail wheel firmly in contact with the tarmac to maintain directional stability. *Frank B. Mormillo*

Below:
U-2R 68-10337 again, this time equipped with a full set of Superpods and antenna protrusions, as seen more often on the TR-1A.
T. Shia (Enterprise Aviation Publications)

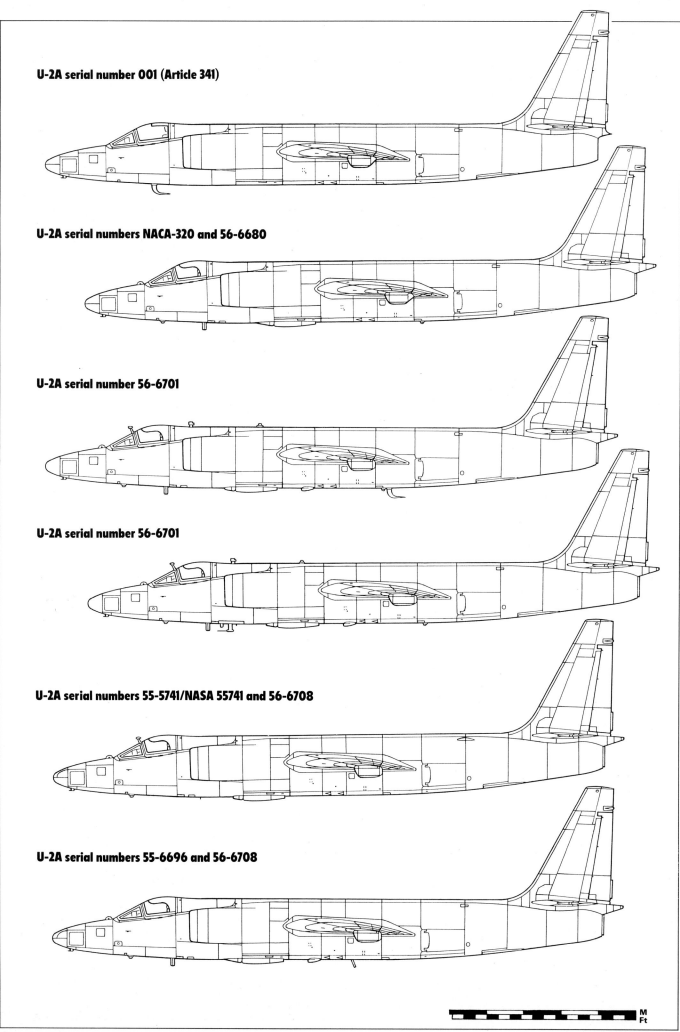

U-2A serial number OO1 (Article 341)

U-2A serial numbers NACA-320 and 56-6680

U-2A serial number 56-6701

U-2A serial number 56-6701

U-2A serial numbers 55-5741/NASA 55741 and 56-6708

U-2A serial numbers 55-6696 and 56-6708

M
Ft

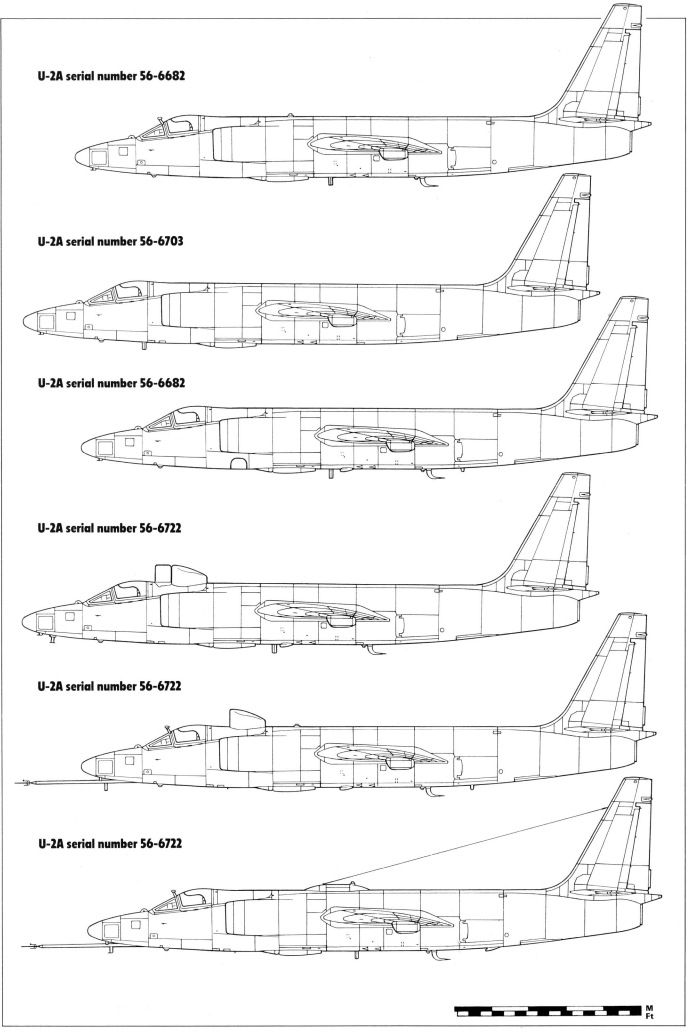

U-2A serial number 56-6682

U-2A serial number 56-6703

U-2A serial number 56-6682

U-2A serial number 56-6722

U-2A serial number 56-6722

U-2A serial number 56-6722

M
Ft

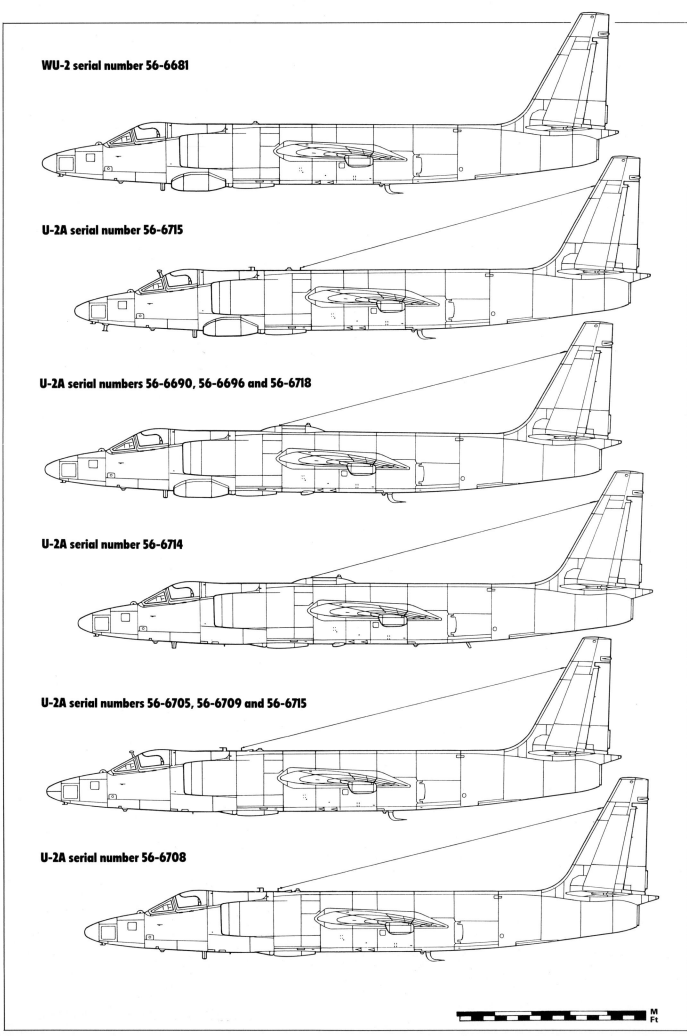

WU-2 serial number 56-6681

U-2A serial number 56-6715

U-2A serial numbers 56-6690, 56-6696 and 56-6718

U-2A serial number 56-6714

U-2A serial numbers 56-6705, 56-6709 and 56-6715

U-2A serial number 56-6708

M
Ft

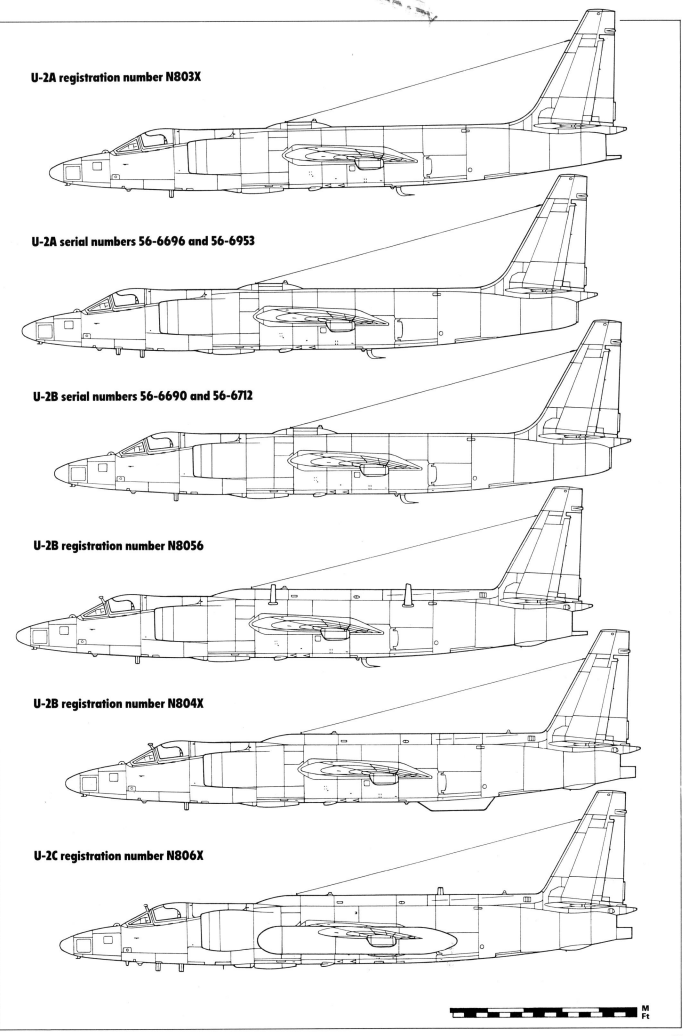

U-2A registration number N803X

U-2A serial numbers 56-6696 and 56-6953

U-2B serial numbers 56-6690 and 56-6712

U-2B registration number N8056

U-2B registration number N804X

U-2C registration number N806X

M
Ft

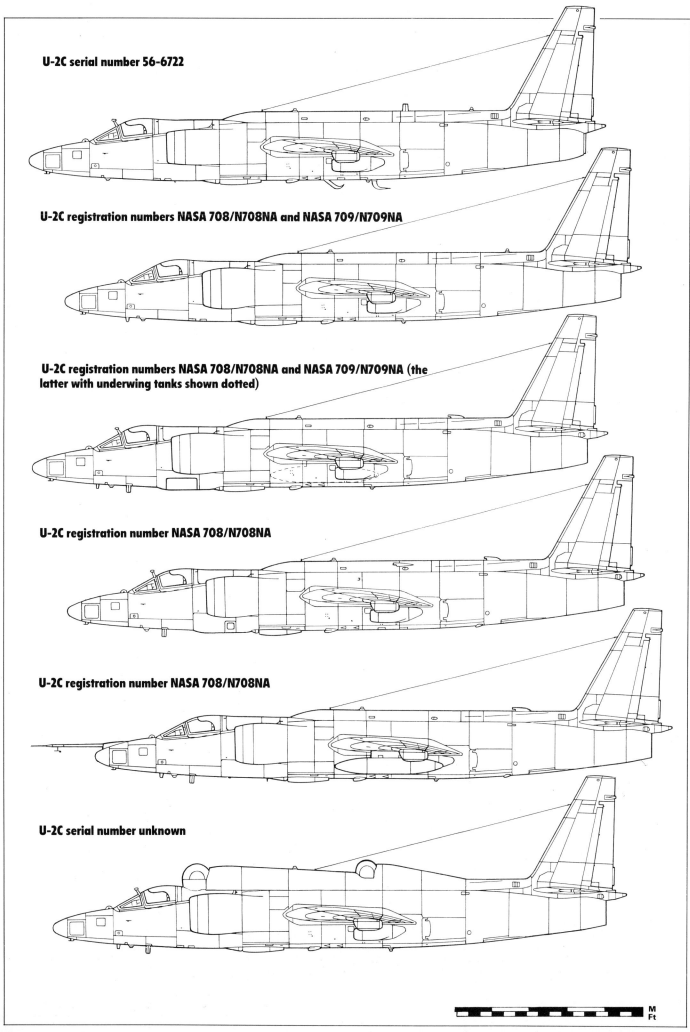

U-2C serial number 56-6722

U-2C registration numbers NASA 708/N708NA and NASA 709/N709NA

U-2C registration numbers NASA 708/N708NA and NASA 709/N709NA (the latter with underwing tanks shown dotted)

U-2C registration number NASA 708/N708NA

U-2C registration number NASA 708/N708NA

U-2C serial number unknown

M
Ft

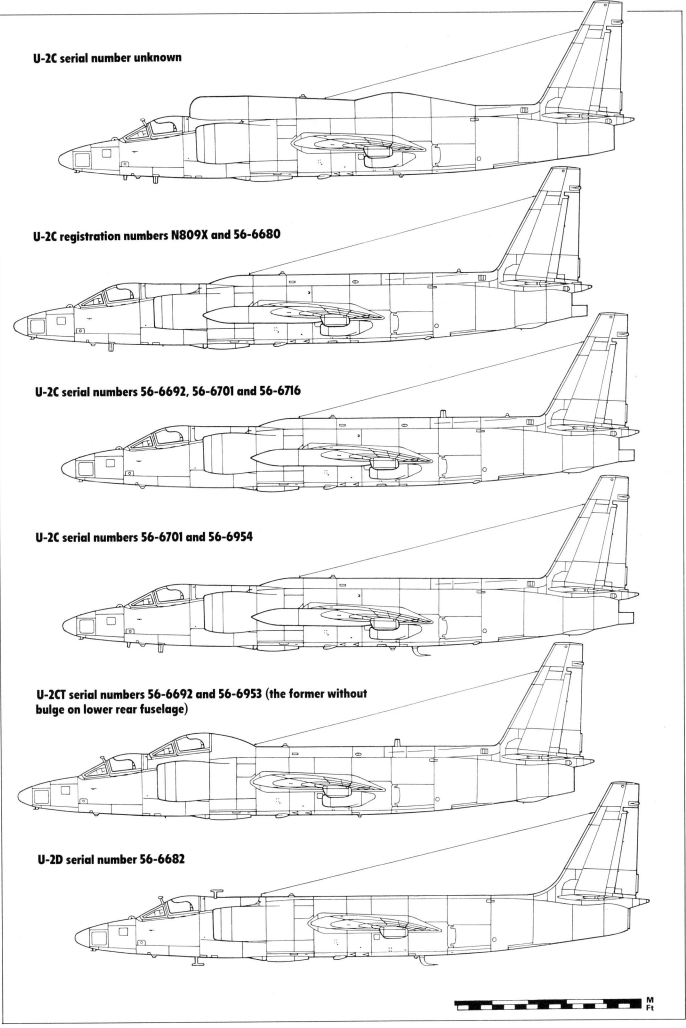

U-2C serial number unknown

U-2C registration numbers N809X and 56-6680

U-2C serial numbers 56-6692, 56-6701 and 56-6716

U-2C serial numbers 56-6701 and 56-6954

U-2CT serial numbers 56-6692 and 56-6953 (the former without bulge on lower rear fuselage)

U-2D serial number 56-6682

M
Ft

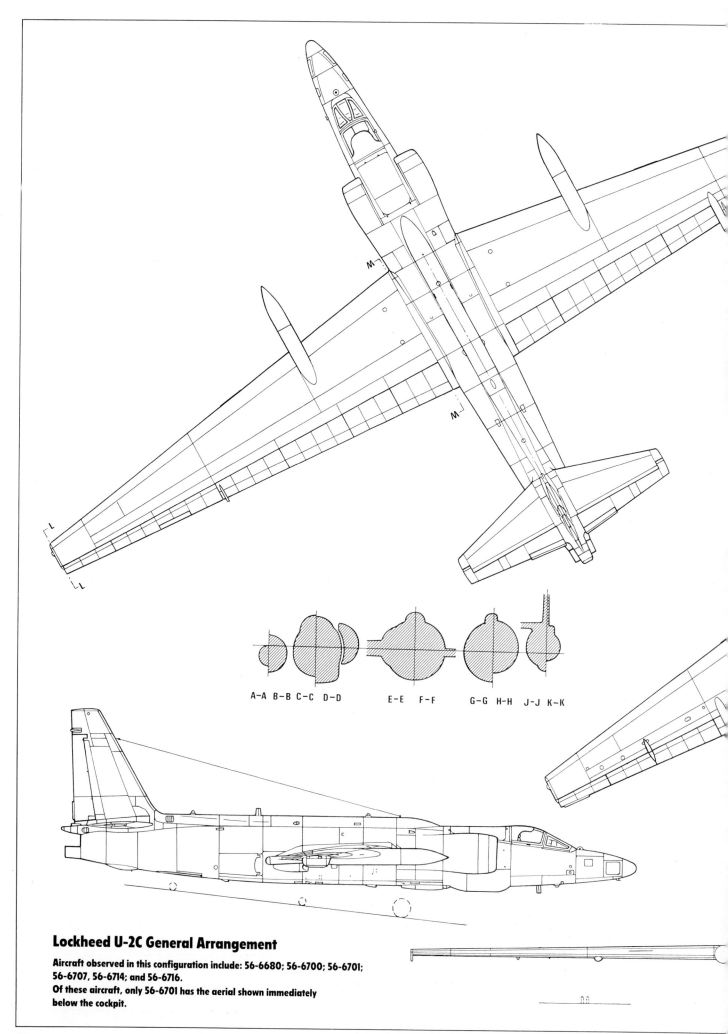

A–A B–B C–C D–D   E–E F–F   G–G H–H J–J K–K

Lockheed U-2C General Arrangement

Aircraft observed in this configuration include: 56-6680; 56-6700; 56-6701;
56-6707, 56-6714; and 56-6716.
Of these aircraft, only 56-6701 has the aerial shown immediately
below the cockpit.

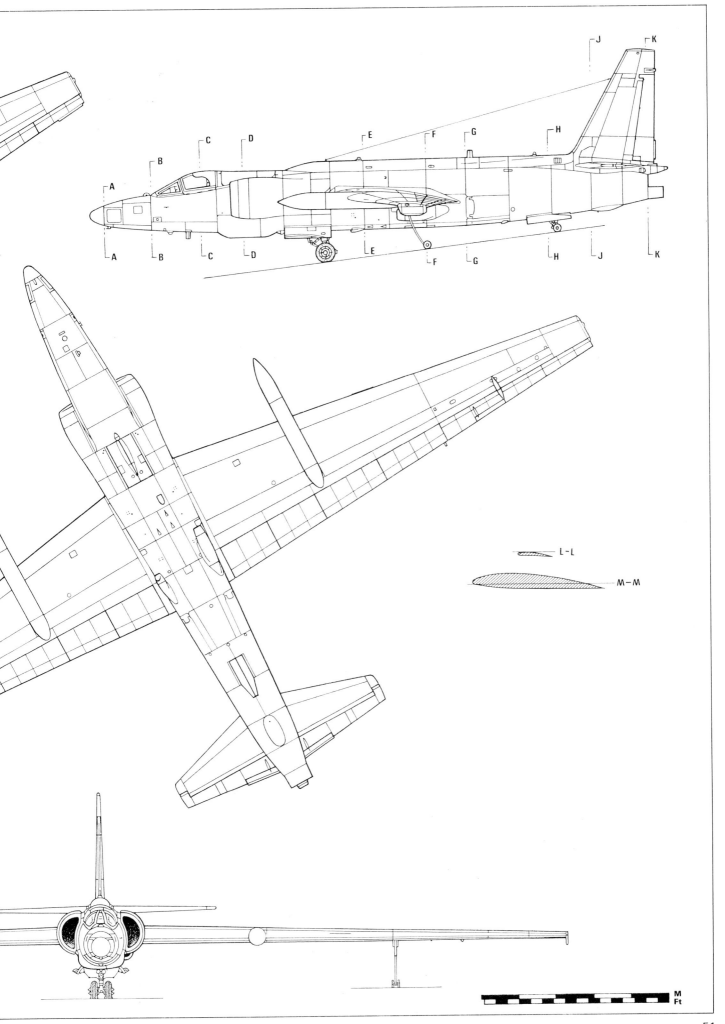

L-L

M-M

M
Ft

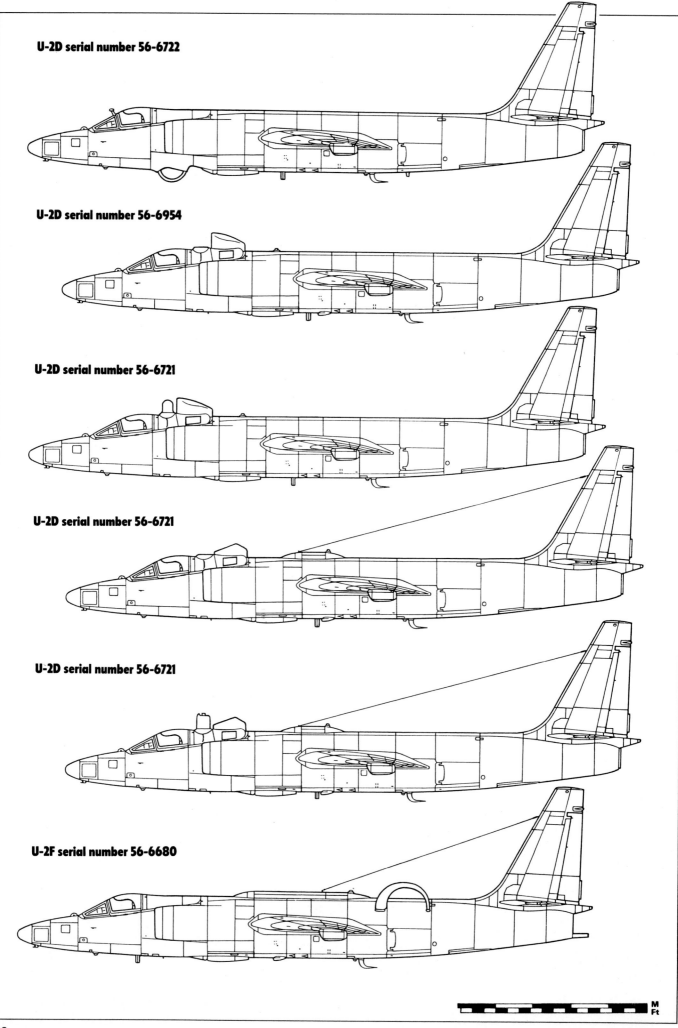

U-2D serial number 56-6722

U-2D serial number 56-6954

U-2D serial number 56-6721

U-2D serial number 56-6721

U-2D serial number 56-6721

U-2F serial number 56-6680

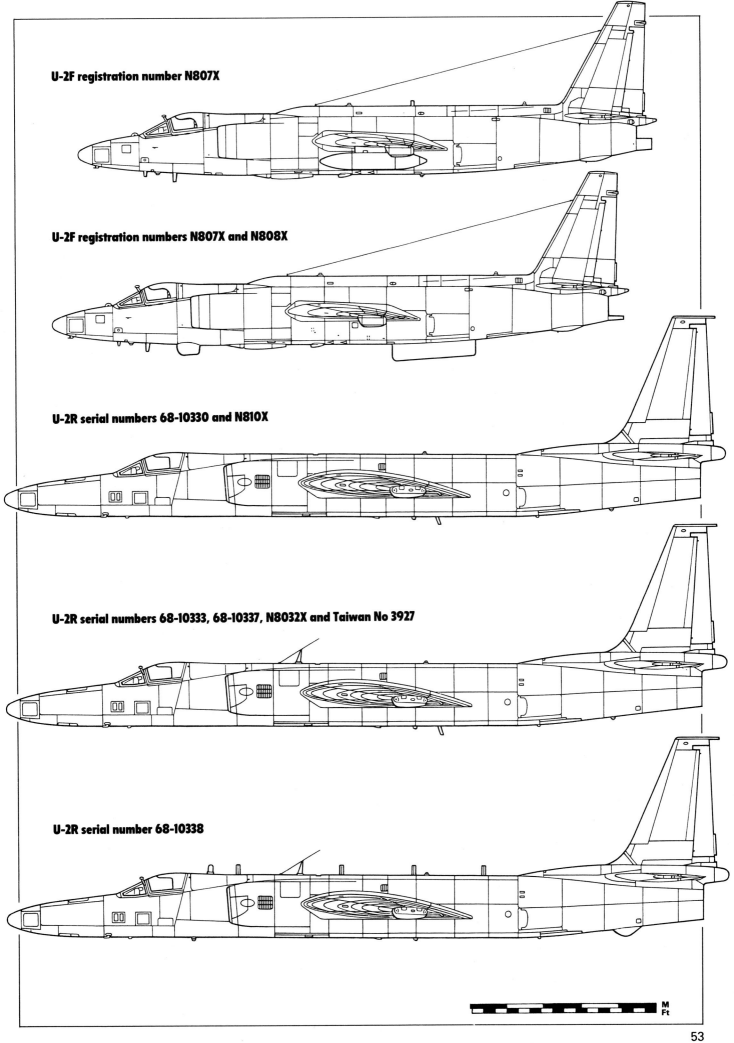

U-2F registration number N807X

U-2F registration numbers N807X and N808X

U-2R serial numbers 68-10330 and N810X

U-2R serial numbers 68-10333, 68-10337, N8032X and Taiwan No 3927

U-2R serial number 68-10338

M
Ft

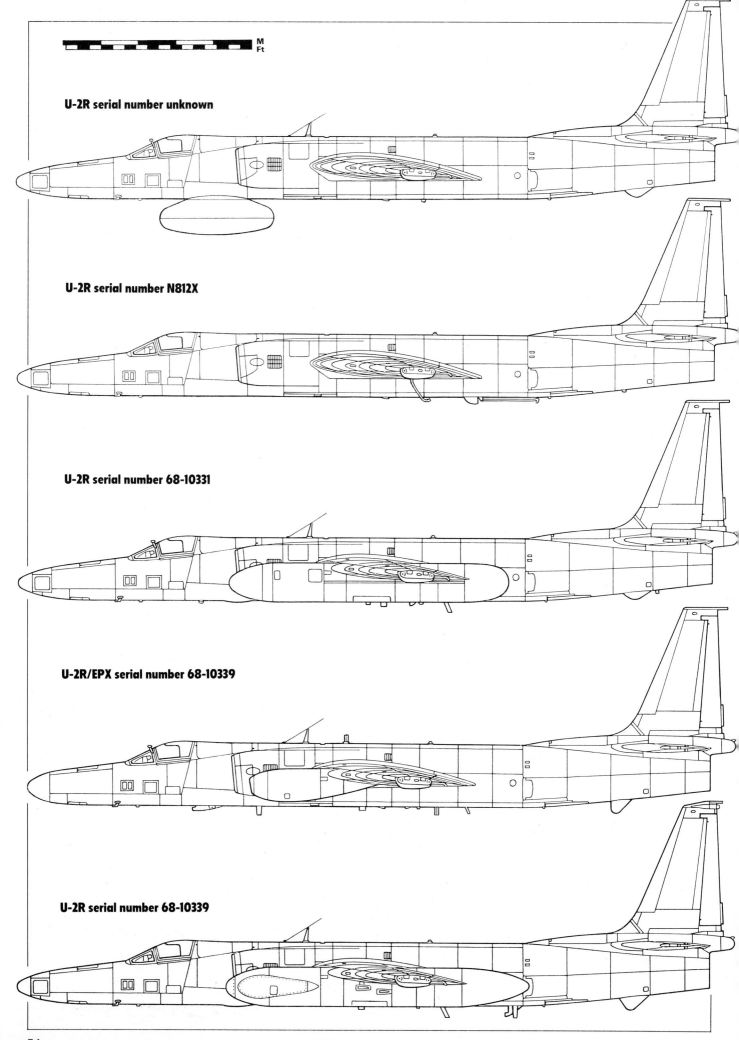

U-2R serial number unknown

U-2R serial number N812X

U-2R serial number 68-10331

U-2R/EPX serial number 68-10339

U-2R serial number 68-10339

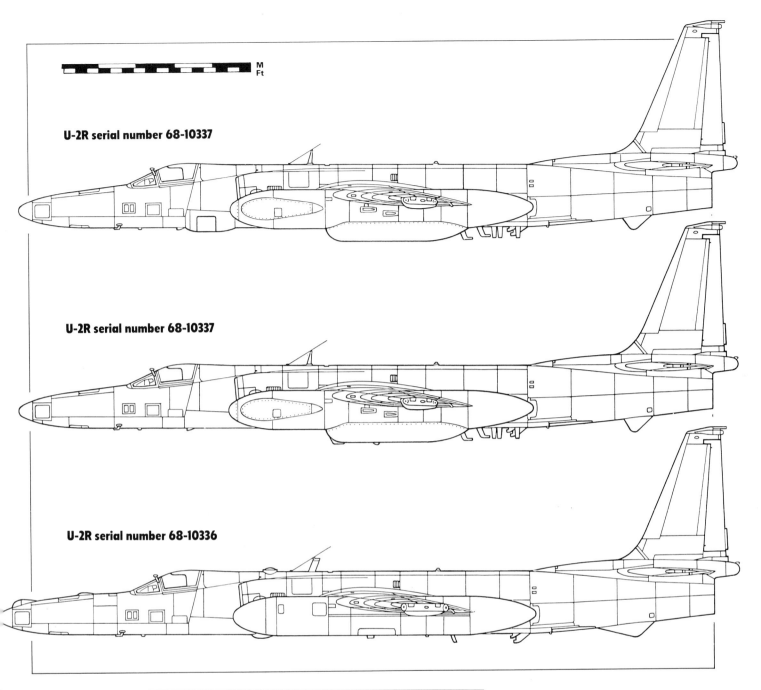

U-2R serial number 68-10337

U-2R serial number 68-10337

U-2R serial number 68-10336

Left:
U-2R 68-10339 displays its aesthetic virtues at their simplest. At other stages in its life, '339 has appeared with Superpods and ASARS-2 nose, conducting TR-1 equipment trials in the UK. It was also the Navy EP-X test-bed.
Lockheed

3
Mini Blackbird

The downing of Francis Gary Powers and his Dragon Lady at the height of the pioneering days of Project 'Oxcart' led to some radical re-thinking on the part of the CIA and Lockheed-California. Although the A-12 and its successor the SR-71 were designed to outrun MiGs and SAMs, the United States had pledged to conduct no more manned overflights of the USSR. The solution therefore seemed relatively simple: build an unmanned remotely-piloted vehicle to do the job instead! Blatant an answer though it was, the Soviet Union had no idea of the advances being made in US drone technology and were quite cocksure that any existing or envisaged RPV could be easily downed as it plied its way obediently on an easy-to-track flightplan. (This was several years before the subsonic Ryan Aeronautical AQM-34 RPVs launched from DC-130s of SAC's 350th SRS, 100th SRW, were to be seen outrunning SA-2s and MiG-21s and displaying incredible audacity by zooming over North Vietnamese airfields at treetop heights to chase MiG jocks off their boarding ladders!) China, also, was proving to be a rapidly growing source of interest to the CIA and DIA.

Lockheed's solution for the strategic mission was a highly secret mini Blackbird, closely resembling a petite A-12 engine nacelle married to an ogival-delta wing. Designated D-21, the RPV was intended to be flown by remote control from a Launch Control Operator (LCO) backseat jury-rigged into the Q-Bay of A-12s 60-6940 and -6941, subsequently referred to as 'Mother Goose' M-12s. Bolted piggyback fashion to a relatively simple pylon on the M-12's dorsal empennage, the D-21 was designed to be launched at speeds above Mach 3, where its Marquardt Co RJ43-MA-11 pure ramjet could spring into life and hoist the drone away for a clandestine Mach 4+ photo-reconnaissance mission through heavily-defended airspace — the knife-like profile of the plastic and titanium D-21, measuring 43·2ft long, and with a modest span of 17ft, presented a target of minimum infra-red and negligible radar signature. Following the high-speed photo pass using a ventral sensor package built into the nacelle, the D-21 would eventually steer to pre-determined co-ordinates programmed into its gyro-navigation gear before the mission, release its film cassette, and then be either self-destructed or retrieved at sea — possibly for reuse, but primarily to prevent it falling into the wrong hands. The USAF states that around 38 D-21s were built between 1964 and early 1969.

The concept was sound, if somewhat expensive, but the M-12/D-21 programme ended in tragedy. Following a series of early captive flight tests, on 30 July 1966 'Mother Goose' 60-6941 took to the air and headed out to the Pacific test range with a fully fuelled-up, 'live' 10-ton D-21 on board. Lockheed test pilot William M. Park was at the helm, engineer Ray Torick in the backseat as LCO; mothership 60-6940 flew chase for the Lockheed-run trial. At the pre-determined release point Ray Torick started up the Marquardt engine and let the RPV go, but it just hovered above the M-12. Caught in the shockwave, the drone bounced back and struck the mothership, which pitched up and snapped like a twig. The test crew ejected successfully from the spiralling nose section but Ray Torick died of water inhalation before he could be saved by Navy medics — an ironic end after the harrowing break-up and high-speed punch-out. It was Bill Park's second unscheduled egress from a Habu (his first was from A-12 60-6939 on 9 July 1964 when the bird's controls locked-up on approach to Groom Lake), and

Right:
Black and titanium mothership 60-6940 with D-21 drone onboard during captive flight-tests in the mid-1960s. The D-21 carries aerodynamic covers on the nose and tail, later removed for the tragic 'live' trial. *USAF*

Left:
A 'Senior Bowl' B-52H equipped with a pair of D-21s. The drones carry ventral booster rockets to propel them to operational heights and cruise speed, to enable the Marquardt ramjet to engage. *Lockheed*

he subsequently transferred over to the up-and-coming U-2R programme. The Blackbird mothership concept was terminated shortly after at Kelly Johnson's own request, despite the inimitable designer's deeply-held conviction that the future of military aviation lay in unmanned vehicles.

With an inventory of some 37 or so expensive near-hypersonic RPVs on hand, the Air Force and its D-21 mentor the CIA looked into alternative modes of launch. The mini Blackbird programme was far from over. A slightly modified D-21B model, complete with revised inlet and strap-on rocket booster, was subsequently redelivered to the 4200th Test Wing, located at Beale AFB, California, for operational trials under the codename 'Senior Bowl'. This force also comprised two B-52H Stratofortress motherships which blended surreptitiously into the 465th Bomb Wing at the base. The B-52Hs could carry two drones at a time, one on each inner wing pylon, and take them up to 45,000ft for launch, the procedures for which had already been successfully perfected by NASA Dryden and the AFFTC Test Force at Edwards AFB, California, during the Rockwell X-15 rocket-plane programme. The jettisonable boosters would then project the RPVs to altitude and speed to permit the Marquardt ramjet to engage, for sustained cruise. Some estimates state a 100,000ft ceiling and a range of 1,250 miles were possible.

Early flights performed off the California coast were designed to perfect launch procedures and film cassette recovery techniques using Mid-Air Retrieval System (MARS)-

equipped Sikorsky helicopters, already in use for Ryan RPV recovery. It has been reported that just under 20 D-21B launches were made from the B-52s, culminating in a handful of operational missions in the war zone in South-East Asia — including China — but 'Senior Bowl' was later abandoned when it was discovered that film cassette recovery proved impractical and unreliable. (One attempt ended in fiasco when the MARS chopper missed the package and a back-up Navy ship — working with the USAF as part of the joint-Service 'Belfrey Express' RPV recovery operations — snagged the parachute line after splash-down, smashing the package against its hull.) Cost considerations, however, were the major factor behind the decision to terminate the operational missions, coupled with improved relations with Communist China following President Nixon's state visit in 1972. (If overflights of the Soviet Union were ever conducted, they are never talked about.) Moreover, the dramatic advances in satellites, sideways-looking radar and oblique camera technology were in the process of making most overflight reconnaissance missions unnecessary. The

remaining D-21Bs were placed in storage by late 1973.

The RPVs next appeared in August 1976 when approximately one dozen were finally taken off the reserve list and airlifted in a pair of C-5A Galaxy transporters to the Davis-Monthan, Arizona-based Military Storage & Disposition Center 'boneyard' under armed guard. These were followed by an additional batch in 1977, bringing the grazing total up to 17 D-21s. Matt black all over and devoid of markings except for a few minor maintenance stencils (the only concessions to identity were tags attached to the wing pitots or white stencils near the inlet lips, bearing numbers in the 503 through 539 serial range), the RPVs later disappeared again in a manner which befitted their mysterious 'black' career. The decision to remove the RPVs was itself classified! Curiously, the red tags on the pitots identified the RPVs as GTD-21Bs, presumably a spin-off from their grounded status, and possibly indicating that some of them may have been used for airframe instruction for fledgling Blackbird groundcrews, and even for high-Mach target practice as drones, or for decoy work. Their exact GTD-21B role remains obscure, but of one thing we can be sure: the D-21s remain as enigmatic as their CIA-operated A-12 sisters; only in the 21st century, when the majority of the crews will have long gone and a few yellowing folders and aluminium film containers stamped 'classified' remain to be opened up, will the full story unfold.

Right:
A rare shot of the D-21's Marquardt Co RJ43-MA-11 ramjet nozzle, set several feet into the exhaust pipe. *Ben Knowles*

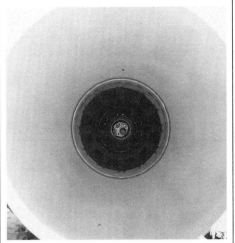

Lockheed A-12/M-12

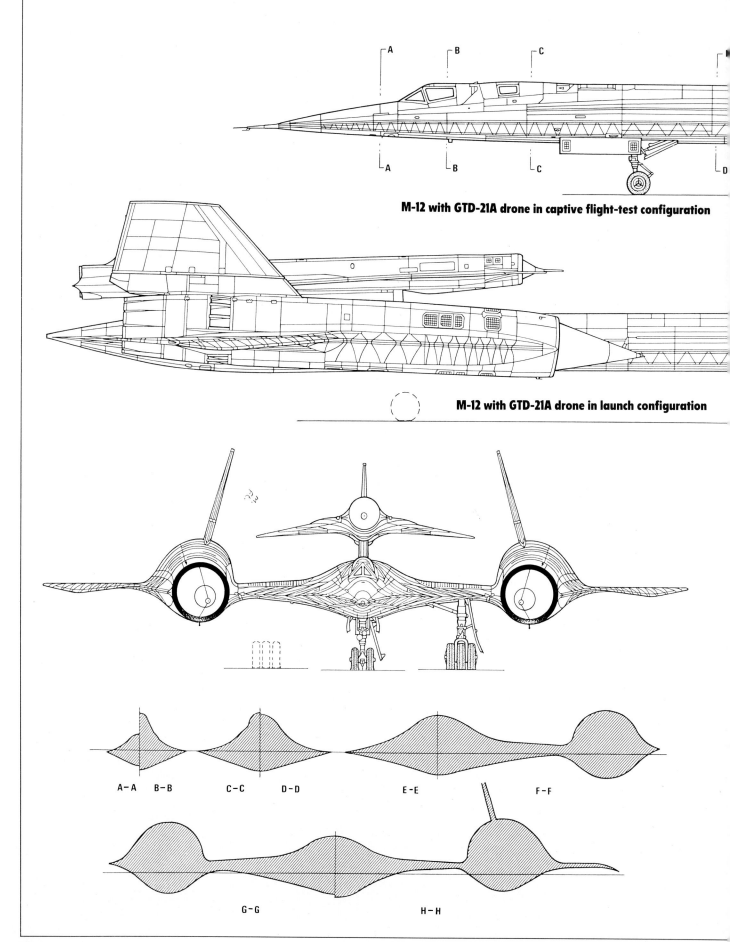

M-12 with GTD-21A drone in captive flight-test configuration

M-12 with GTD-21A drone in launch configuration

A-A B-B C-C D-D E-E F-F

G-G H-H

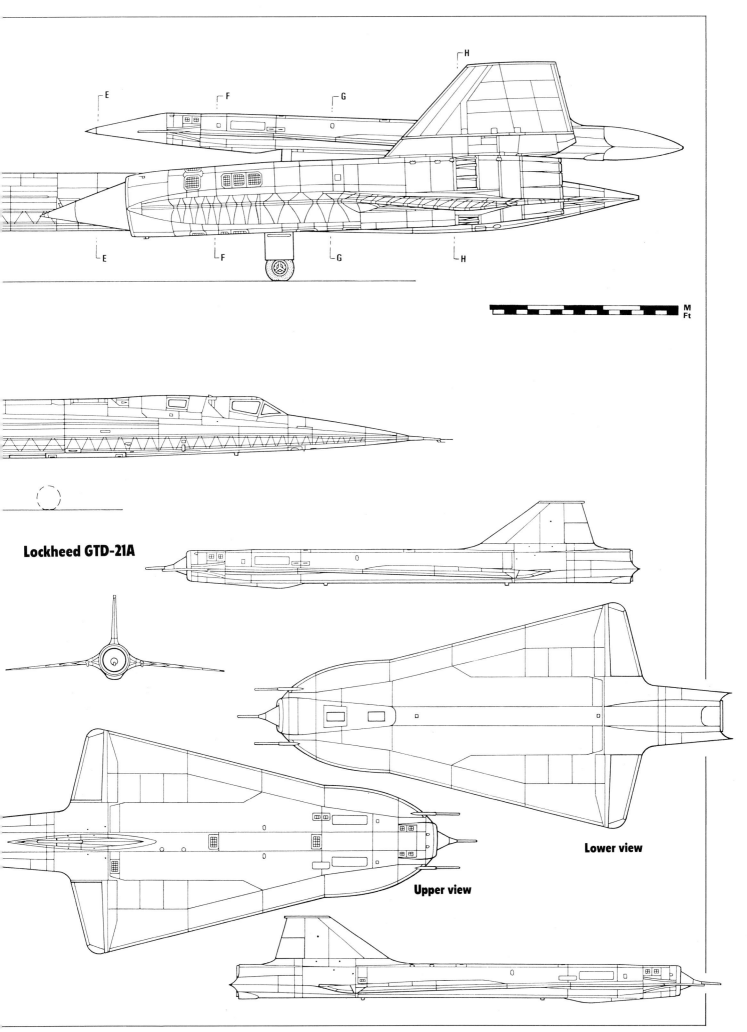

Lockheed GTD-21A

Lower view

Upper view

Lockheed M-12

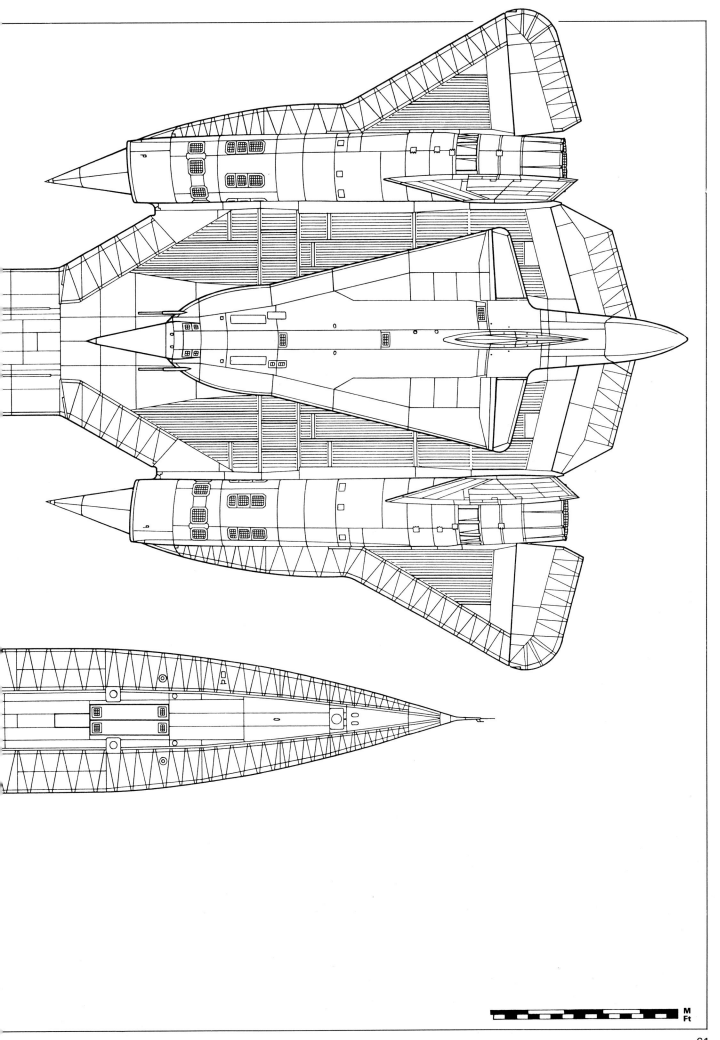

4
Beale –
'Tamers' and 'Charmers'

Top:
'Like a snake swallowing three mice when seen head on' was how Kelly Johnson described his masterpiece. SR-71A 64-17974, formerly known as 'Ichi Ban', taxies on to March AFB's main runway in November 1981.
Frank B. Mormillo

'We love it here. We know you will too.' So reads the slogan of an estate agent near Beale AFB, California. Citizens who fail to derive real pleasure from the apocalyptic din of an SR-71 take-off might disagree, but the place certainly recommends itself to lovers of exotic flying machines. The 12-mile road from Marysville, the nearest town, leads to the hub of SAC's Strategic Reconnaissance 14th Air Division (AD), controlling the 9th SRW — the Blackbird flyers.

This territory's original owner, Gen Edward F. Beale, had a taste for the unorthodox himself. He fought alongside folk-hero Kit Carson in the Mexican Wars, becoming Super-intendent of Indian Affairs for the California and New Mexico area. To provide effective military transport in the arid terrain he imported sufficient animals to form the Army Camel Corps. When the US Army dropped his novel plan Gen Beale herded the redundant ruminants back to his ranch and kept them as pets. Later, he became Surveyor-General for the region, occupying his spare time by purchasing ranches with foreclosed mortgages and eventually became the largest landowner in California. President Lincoln remarked that he had appointed Beale Surveyor-General, though he now understood that Gen Beale was 'monarch of all he has surveyed' — a comment which applies in some sense to the current inhabitants of Beale's Blackbird 'barns' — the TR-1/U-2R and SR-71.

In 1942, 86,000 acres of this real estate became Camp Beale, although no runways were set out until 1957. The first KC-135 of the 456th BW arrived in July 1959, and the 14th AD was established in January 1960, administering the Stratotankers, three new B-52 Wings, plus an element of Titan missiles. The association with strategic reconnais-sance began on 1 January 1965 when the 4200th SRW was established to

Top:
Tucking up its gear, 64-17964 leaves March AFB in October 1979. The aircraft is as long as a Boeing 737 airliner.
Frank B. Mormillo

Above:
Aircraft 64-17975 pulls away from Norton AFB at an impressive angle after a touch-and-go. In place of the Skunk emblem, '975 wore a black cat with white whiskers (as seen on U-2R 68-10331) during its 1981 stint with Kadena's 9th SRW Det 1.
Frank B. Mormillo

pave the way for SR-71 operations, using eight T-38A trainers. Their first Habu checked in 53 weeks later and the Wing became operational as the 9th SRW on 22 June 1966 under Col Douglas T. Nelson. Lt-Col William R. Griner commanded the 1st Strategic Reconnaissance Squadron, which took over the designation of the original US military flying unit, the 1st Aero Squadron. (In 1913 the

9th SRW Detachments

Det 1   Kadena AB, Okinawa, Japan
Det 2   Osan AB, South Korea
Det 3   RAF Akrotiri, Cyprus
Det 4   RAF Mildenhall, Suffolk, England
Det 5   Patrick AFB, Florida, USA
Det 6   Palmdale, California, USA

Present U-2R and SR-71 operations are conducted out of up to 20 OLs, under the authority of the 9th SRW and its Detachment bases, scattered worldwide. Palmdale is responsible for follow-on research and development work, while permanent SR-71A Det bases are confined to Nos 1 and 4 only. Det 4 no longer operates the U-2R.

Main Operating Units

1st	SRS	SR-71A/B*		
5th	SRTS	U-2CT, TR-1A/B	9th SRW	Beale AFB, California, USA
99th	SRS	U-2R		
95th	RS	TR-1A	17th RW	RAF Alconbury, England

*A solitary SR-71C trainer, 64-17981, may be rotated back into service from storage when the single remaining SR-71B, 64-17956, goes in for deep maintenance.

unit's Curtiss Flyer performed the first recorded reconnaissance flight for Gen Pershing's 2nd Army.) The 9th Wing itself has a creditable history stretching back to 1922 when it incorporated the 1st, 5th and 99th Squadrons as the 9th Observation Group. Varying duties over the next half-century saw it operating the MB-2 bomber, the B-17, B-29 and B-47; Stratojet operations ended in 1966 at Mountain Home AFB, Idaho, when the 9th decamped to Beale.

The Wing then regained its old 99th Squadron. This title was applied to the 349th SRS in July 1976, when it moved its U-2s in from Davis-Monthan to join the 1st SRS; the A-7D programme at Davis-Monthan, not to mention TAC's newly acquired DC-130A/E RPV motherships there, were making it tough for U-2 drivers to conduct their ponderous landing procedures in a sky full of SLUFs and Herks. Confusingly, the 99th had been Beale's second SR-71 unit from June 1966 until 1 April 1971. As originally envisaged, the SAC SR-71 programme, 'Senior Crown', required two parallel squadrons of 20 crews each, but high costs prevented expansion to that extent, and the 99th label was subsequently transferred to the 100th SRW at OL-20, the unit controlling U-2 operations in South-East Asia. It returned to Davis-Monthan in 1976 and thence, by degrees, to Beale AFB from March onwards, to re-adopt its late wartime designation. In re-uniting the 1st and 99th, a partnership dating back to World War 1 was re-activated — but the Lockheed jets flew rather differently from the Sopwith Camels issued to the unit then! To add to the exclusiveness of the high-flying club, Beale's sole remaining 17th BW B-52s thundered off as the U-2s glided in, and in 1983 the 100th ARW's KC-135Qs were absorbed into the 9th, giving the Wing a clear run on its base.

Beale's position as a centre of the strategic intelligence business was consolidated by the installation of its huge AN/FPS-115 Pave Paws radar in 1979, enabling satellites and sea-launched ballistic missiles to be monitored. Today, Beale operates on a 23,000-acre site with around 4,500

personnel and an annual payroll of over $100 million — big money, even to Gen Beale. Incidentally, although that pioneering gentleman's camels are no longer a problem, cows can be. A KC-135Q ran into a herd on the runway in 1977, overshot and burned out.

5th SRTS

Essentially, the 9th SRW exists to provide aircrew and support for SAC's U-2/TR-1 and SR-71 activities worldwide. Its current Dragon Lady training programme is centred on the 5th Strategic Reconnaissance Training Squadron. This squadron number is another link with the 9th Wing's 'heavy bombing' past, but its revival was delayed when it was decided to use one of the old 4080th SRW squadron designations for the TR-1 training unit instead. In August 1981 the 4029th SRTS assumed this job, taking the name 'Dragon Tamers'. In July 1983 it also absorbed the SR-71 training function, but in 1986 it became the 5th SRTS after all — with the exclusive task of preparing U-2/TR-1 flyers.

Col John H. Storrie, commanding the 9th SRW at the time of the 1976 merger, saw the move as a cost-

cutter but welcomed the Dragon jockeys. Along with several of his SR-71 crew colleagues he checked out in a U-2CT to underline the unitary role of the Wing. Concentrating the training in a single unit also reflected the many similarities in mission and support procedures. Both high-flying Blackbird types require the same suiting-up, pre-flight routine. U-2 pilots dress in the S1010B suit while their Habu colleagues use the very similar S1030, regarded by Kelly Johnson as an 'escape capsule in itself'. For both aircraft types, pilots and RSOs are volunteers who submit themselves to a gruelling selection procedure. In 1980, for example, half the applicants failed the initial screening and only 10% were finally accepted. Apart from the periodic depredations resulting from airline recruitment

Left:
'Pave Onyx' U-2C 56-6714 at Davis-Monthan AFB, Arizona in 1976. The unusual two-tone grey 'Sabre' scheme was sprayed on in 1975 to allay UK government anxieties during the Wethersfield deployment — the more regular black paintwork was considered to be far too provocative because of its 'black' bird associations with the aircraft's CIA spyplane past. This machine was damaged in 1980 when it clipped power lines at Oroville, California, and was subsequently patched-up and put on display at Beale. *Mick Roth via Ben Knowles*

Above:
U-2C 56-6682, once used for carrier trials by the CIA, served with NASA at Ames from 1971. It is seen here in July 1987. *Jeff Puzzullo/AIR*

Left:
Converted into the U-2CT two-seat trainer configuration in 1976, 56-6692 basks in the California sun with 'howdah' sunshades keeping the cockpit cool. *MAP*

there is seldom a shortage of applicants. Crews emerge from a variety of backgrounds. Half the original batch of 10 Habu men were fresh from SAC's hot B-58 Hustler, and candidates continued to appear from SAC heavy bomber units to some extent. Maj Bob Uebelacker, TR-1A pilot and ex-bomber jock, explained to the authors that no particular aircraft provided the ideal background for Blackbird command. Maj Steve Randle, also on TR-1As, commented that it is 'a fairly masochistic thing to do to fly the TR-1, so it probably takes a unique motivation for each individual who decides he wants to do it'. There may also be a distinctive attitude among potential crew which has led to them being described as 'the last of the individualists'. Steve Randle agreed that their job is 'a bit less structured than the rest of our brothers in SAC. We aren't tethered quite so much as to direction from HQ like the bomber and tanker people

are. We're capable of going off by ourselves without being under constant supervision. And if people don't live up to that we come down on them — hard!' The small size of the recon community also marks out individuality.

Things would be much the same for SR-71 candidates, except that their mission involves a team effort. Habu men work as a pair and the partnership is normally preserved for the standard three-to-four-year tour of duty, though many stay longer. (Maj Thom Evans, with nine years on U-2R/TR-1, was the high-timer in 1984.) Steve Randle explained: 'People tend to stay, as a generalisation, in most cases up to retirement. A main reason for this is that they start (on U-2/TR-1) at "career middle-age", because we need people with so much flying experience. By the time you take a pilot who has done a reasonable amount of time on the programme to

Right:
During its second visit to Alconbury in February 1985, TR-1B 01065 flew proficiency check-flights most days, including practice approaches to Lakenheath and Wethersfield. An initial three-week deployment was made in March 1984 to test the cost-effectiveness of on-base training at Alconbury rather than Beale.
Peter R. Foster

Below:
Displaying its huge wing, copious flap area and odd landing gear, U-2R 68-10377 heads for the Davis-Monthan runway just before the 349th SRS moved to Beale in July 1976.
Frank B. Mormillo

Far left:
Col 'Silver Fox' Stephens and his FCO, Maj Daniel Andre, exchange the customary handshake during the 1 May 1965 record-breaking series of sorties they flew with YF-12A 60-6936, behind. The bird lacks its chin-mounted infra-red sensors, deleted on '6936 to reduce drag during the altitude and speed record-setting sorties. *USAF*

Top left:
The YF-12A set a whole catalogue of world speed and altitude records on 1 May 1965. The white stencils on the nose indicate XAIM-47A missile launches. '936 was lost on approach after a fuel fire on 24 June 1971.
Don Spering/AIR

Centre left:
A GTD-21B 'mini Blackbird' drone sits on its transport dolly at Davis-Monthan AFB, Arizona in September 1978.
Ben Knowles

Below:
NASA's YF-12C was actually the prototype SR-71A (64-17951). After extensive development work at Edwards AFB it was put into long-term storage at Palmdale in 1978. This is a 1979 shot. *Don Spering/AIR*

pay back the training, he's getting a little old to go on to something else'.

Similar sentiments are expressed in the SR-71 community which has also produced some high-time pilots of tremendous experience. Among the initial cadre of aircrew was Robert Powell, an experienced U-2 pilot who became the high-time SR-71 driver on his retirement as Lieutenant-Colonel in February 1974. He had to wait a year in the 4200th SRW before there was a Habu seat for him to fill. This time was usefully spent in the simulator whenever possible (a luxury denied to U-2 pilots then and now). He went on to log a final total of 1,020 hours and over a million miles. On one occasion he suffered a double flame-out. The 5min glide while he orchestrated re-starts was marked chiefly by 'panic, terror and what have you'. Eventually, he could line up 17 Air Medals and two DFCs, with more Mach 3+ hours in his book than any other pilot in the world.

By 1981 other SR-71 crews were beginning to rack up considerable flight hours — no mean achievement when one considers that their speed-of-heat sorties are quite short in relation to the effort involved in laying on a flight in the complex Blackbird. George T. Morgan was the

first RSO to beat 1,000 hours (one fifth of it 'combat' time) in a career which enabled the much-decorated Lt-Col Morgan to become Chief of Flight Test Ops at Palmdale. While at Beale he had the distinction of actually wearing out his tailor-made pressure suit, which had 14 patches on it by the time it was binned. Morgan was also RSO to Capt Eldon W. Joersz for the World Speed Record flight of 28 July 1976 when a figure of 2,193.16mph appeared on the record books — and stayed there.

The accumulation of high flight hour totals on the SR-71 is certainly more difficult than it is in the current range of switch-on-and-fly jets. Each of the current SR-71s usually averages less than 200 hours per year. Beale's operational crews get three-to-four Habu flights a month with around six sorties in one of the 14 T-38A proficiency trainers. The rest of their cockpit time is in the simulator. However, like their U-2 stablemates, crews also act as mobile officers and standby crew for their squadron on a

rota basis. A spare crew usually briefs alongside the designated mission crew, though the chances are that participation will actually only be made from the chase car supervising the take-off and landing procedures.

These precautions have contributed to the SR-71's excellent safety record in 9th SRW use. After a predictably difficult start in its test programme, the hottest and most complex of Blackbirds now has a long reputation for looking after its crews, despite some spectacular accidents! Of those beasts relegated to scrap, aircraft 64-17977 got there by ending its career in flames after skidding 1,000ft off the south end of Beale's runway on 10 October 1968; take-off had to be aborted after wheel failure in one of the main undercarriage trucks, but both crew escaped. Tail number 64-17957, the second SR-71B trainer, crashed on 11 January that same year, having stalled on approach and 'fluttered to the ground like a feather', according to eye-witnesses. Both instructor and student landed by parachute and sat somewhat ignominiously in an old chicken ranch awaiting retrieval while the expensive Blackbird flopped down inverted in a nearby field at Loma Rica. The cause was double generator failure exacerbated by a double flame-out and the crew had made a superb effort to recover the aircraft with only minutes' worth of battery power at their disposal for the — as it turned out, no-go — chance of a re-start. On a more sombre note, there was no fatal SR-71 crew accident at Beale until Maj James Hudson died after ejecting at insufficient altitude in an aborted T-38A take-off. To date, this is still the only fatal accident and there has been no SR-71 loss since the demise of 'Rapid Rabbit' in 1973. Despite tanker collisions (64-17970, lost in 1970), engine

Top:
T-38A 64-13190, nicknamed 'Joycie', sits on the ramp at Beale AFB in company with the 9th SRW's other T-38s, and KC-135Qs. The Talon companion trainers are some of the busiest jets at the base. *MAP*

Above:
TR-1A 80-1067, the 9th SRW's second example, at Edwards AFB in October 1982. The basic Superpods have vent holes at each end to avoid pressure build-up. Pilots use the mirror which protrudes from the canopy bow to check for fuel venting and contrail formation. *Frank B. Mormillo*

fires (64-17964 'Skyshark', recovered in June 1987) and a host of un-start, pitch-up and stall incidents, the guys tend to get home.

A basic requirement for the numerous applicants to the SR-71/TR-1/U-2R programme is 1,500 hours flying time (with 750 hours as aircraft commander). In the late 1960s those figures were 2,000 and 1,500 hours respectively — the same as for the astronaut programme. Up to 10 years ago, U-2 candidates needed 2,500 hours in three different types. Although the baseline has been relaxed a little, most candidates tend

to offer as many as 3,000 hours in any case. Top physical condition is a prerequisite, though this too — and the ability to tolerate the constraints of long, high flights — is less stringently tested than in the astronaut 'superman' days. Crews therefore endure a series of interviews to establish their psychological aptitude, willingness to work in the team (no 'Top Gun' Maverick clones here, thank you!) and — of course — security clearance. These qualities and the ability to *manage* systems correctly are just as important as flying skills. The 1st SRS normally inducts about three new crew per year, while recruitment to the expanding TR-1 community has been a little higher.

Once the selectors have decided that SAC can invest a year's training in an individual the demanding process begins. Currently the 5th SRTS gives its TR-1 'learners' an initial phase of five lo-altitude sorties in a two-seater, with a subsequent check-ride. The emphasis here is on the problems of landing technique. Then there is a hi-altitude TR-1B flight, followed by eight other 'hi' sorties and another evaluative check. TR-1

Below:
Being hauled off the ramp at Andrews AFB is SR-71A 17960 in 1984-style featureless black. Other Lockheed products at lower Mach ratings can be seen in the background.
Don Spering/AIR

Left:
A lovely Don Spering shot of the only two-seater in the game, 64-17956, at Beale in 1975. This variant lacks operational capability but scores well on sinister aesthetics. *Don Spering/AIR*

Right:
SR-71A 64-17971 stands on display in the hot California sun. Note the nose-up attitude of the fuselage relative to the engine nacelles. *USAF*

pilots who are scheduled for the overseas unit, the 95th RS in England, will then be sent over for local familiarisation. Those who opt for Beale's eight or nine U-2Rs have to accumulate 100 hours on type before being allowed a TDY to one of the overseas FOLs — as do SR-71 crews. The two U-2CT trainers are still used and in the absence of a simulator they have played a vital, though much belated, role in the training regime since 1972, when U-2CT 56-6953 was delivered. It is still '953 which flies most often (despite the retirement of the early U-2Cs with which it was partnered), though companion hump-back 56-6692 was still at Beale in 1987. This second U-2CT arrived in 1976, further reducing the severe attrition of U-2s in training. Accidents tended to occur most frequently in a new pilot's first three landings and the presence of an instructor greatly eased this problem. Originally, two-seat experience was provided with an assortment of borrowed T-33s. Pilots then went solo on U-2 right away. Wash-out is low, with the 5th SRTS preferring, instead, to spend more time polishing an individual rather than taking on another, complete novice. Not so long ago two bad landings meant being kicked out of the system — or 'the program' as crews refer, somewhat affectionately, to their high-flying career. As one experienced Staff pilot put it: That's why we have three interview rides . . . if he can't handle that we don't waste the money training him.'

SR-71 pilots use their back-up jet, the T-38A, to evaluate new pilots. Seemingly irreplaceable throughout the USAF, the supersonic T-38A is a vital tool in 9th SRW business. It acts as chase aircraft for Habus returning from sorties and has been the companion trainer for the SR-71 since July 1965. Dressed in white, the T-38A Talons carry the 9th SRW's four Maltese crosses, signifying World War 1 service, on a yellow tail band. Recently they have all begun to carry names such as 'Battlecat' (13270), 'Joycie' (13190), 'White Shark' (00581) and the more puzzling 'Wind Breaker' (13297) on their sleek noses. The Talon's subsonic handling characteristics are very similar to

those of the larger SR-71, with slightly lighter stick forces and faster response rates. The only drawback from the Habu drivers' point of view is that the aircraft are pooled by the Wing, and one can also find U-2 pilots in the Talons' cockpits making up their hours and occasionally even tanker pilots from the 9th SRW's two resident KC-135Q squadrons, the 349th ARS and 350th ARS, leaving the SR-71 fraternity with less time on the T-38 than they would like. Maj Dan House, a dedicated Blackbird flyer who flew the Dragon Lady and who is now current on the Habu, commented: 'The T-38 came to Beale AFB originally to augment flying time for SR-71 crews and the jet is about as

perfect a companion trainer as one could hope for. The T-38 subsequently got flown by the U-2 pilots, who moved to Beale in 1976. The U-2 and T-38 are not similar in any way that I can think of except they both go into the air and eventually come back down. The Beale T-38s are also flown by the Wing staff and by tanker co-pilots in the ACE (accelerated co-pilot enrichment) program. The T-38 is *so much* fun to fly that I suspect we will never get the Wing staff or co-pilots out of them so that the SR crews can get the time they need to stay proficient in the air!'

Pilots in the 1st SRS make up a great deal of time in the unique SR-71 simulator, which is also employed in

Right:
One of Lockheed photographer Bob Ferguson's lyrical studies of the first TR-1B, 80-1064, off the California coast. *Lockheed*

Above:
Fireball Express. At the 'speed of heat' even the serial is illegible. *Lockheed*

Below:
A tail-first tow for U-2R 68-10337 and two external passengers. This model introduced a zero-zero seat, stronger landing gear, an increase in fuel capacity, all-moving tail, and a substantially redesigned basic airframe. This particular U-bird was the last U-2R to operate the regular Mildenhall detachment, where it was a frequent visitor between 1981 and 1983.
Frank B. Mormillo

the selection stage. Equipped with the same old-fashioned instrument dials as the real thing (except that Habu dials have a matt glass finish to cut glare), the Habu 'sim' has no external displays through its windows so all 'flying' is on those instruments. However, the noise of afterburner ignition, the sensation of tyres bumping over runway joins and rotation angle on take-off are all reproduced.

Selecting candidates for the SR-71 programme is a tough job, even more so than that for the TR-1/U-2R. Dan House explained why: 'We are so small a unit that it is impossible to say if one type of background makes a better crew. The critical difference between an average "excellent" crew, and one that stands a little above, is how well they work together. We normally don't find this out for sure until a crew is half-way through training. I suppose that ideally an SR-71 candidate would have flown at least two or three different airplanes, mostly high per-

formance types. He should have experience working with a crew, air refuelling, and operating at high altitude. There is no one out there like this, so we take the best we can get, of course. Many crews have F/FB-111 experience, though this is more a result of the personnel and assignment system than anything else, in my opinion.'

New pilots receive around 100 hours (originally 150) in the 'sim', with five rides in the two-seat SR-71B fitted into the later stages. Flight refuelling and supersonic flight are tackled early in the series, while night flying is introduced on the fourth flight. After the final check-ride a pilot is cleared for six rides in the SR-71A, the sixth being a recent addition (as in the TR-1 programme). Switching from the 'B' to the 'A' model presents no problems; both share a common front seat and handle almost identically, though the instructor's station in the back of the trainer is 'cramped and harder to see out of'. However, the most significant differences

Right:
SR-71 A64-17975 displays its clean lines during a pass over Norton AFB in November 1979. *Frank B. Mormillo*

Below right:
Connected to the old air starters at Mildenhall, 64-17972 is given the once-over by Habu crew and a privileged tech-rep. The Buick V8 600hp air starters were later supplemented by more powerful, reliable Chevrolet starters which are still used for launches out in the open or at remote FOLs. *MAP*

students, instructors and operational crews alike are likely to face are the idiosyncracies of the individual aircraft. Dan House: 'they are all different, and the same plane will act differently from day to day. We all have our favourite tail numbers and the ones we consider problem children.' Once cleared on the 'A' model the new pilot is teamed with an RSO and the pair take their 'for better or worse' vows in the arranged marriage and stay together in the programme from then on. The RSO will have trained to operate his sensor, ECM and communications equipment in a separate simulator, spending relatively more time there than in the air. He normally has 13 four-hour 'Qual' sessions before flying the real machine. After a further check-ride the duo are eligible for mission-ready status. As more hours are clocked up, they go on to attain 'R' (ready for operations) level, then 'E' (senior) standard, and, eventually, 'S' (select) status, at which point these 'old heads' take charge of the Dets, oversee Standardisation/Evaluation (Stan/Eval or aircrew 'quality control') and the vetting of new candidates wishing to enter the programme.

The majority of SR-71 flying from Beale is for crew training and the nature of the machine and its mission mean that the training regime is among the most demanding in the whole Air Force. Decisions have to be made fast at Mach 3+ and there are no second chances or opportunities to relax during a mission. As the old Beale motto has it, 'You've never been lost until you're lost at Mach 3'. The 9th SRW's excellent safety record in recent years shows that rigorous routines pay off. It is also a tribute to the support organisations at Beale which keep their rare aviary in good health and plumage. Ben Rich summed up their responsibilities neatly: 'The men and women of SAC meticulously maintain (the SR-71s). They must. At altitudes above 80,000ft and speeds of over Mach 3 the smallest problem would be disastrous for their two-man crews.'

Right:
A near white-hot J58 (P&W designation JT11D-20B) undergoing running tests.
Pratt & Whitney

Logistics

Beale's Blackbird fixers work in several units. The 9th Organizational Maintenance Squadron (OMS) handles day-to-day servicing, inspection, minor repairs and launch and recovery. Heavier maintenance on all the Wing's aircraft falls to the 9th Field Maintenance Squadron (FMS) which provides intermediate level repairs and refurbishment. Personnel with the initials 'FMS' on their caps can be found repacking parachutes, or lubricating or replacing parts on anything from an SR-71 to a KC-135Q. Most of Beale's birds are noted for the complexity of their avionics and these are kept on line by the 9th Avionics Maintenance Squadron (AMS). Sensors, navigation, communications and ECM packages are tweaked and preened in the Precision Measurement Equipment Laboratory. The 9th AMS's staff also deal with the simulators for SR-71 and KC-135Q and the T-10 navigation trainer. A further vital function is provided by the 9th Reconnaissance Technical Squadron (RTS). Blackbird missions generate a torrent of data. This is controlled and interpreted at the 9th RTS or in their Mobile Processing Center vans which are normally located in hangars at the FOLs. Suitably transcribed or printed up as glossies, the information is in turn passed on to the relevant customer. Further scrutiny of magnetic Elint data is performed at the most secret of SAC establishments: the 544th Strategic Intelligence Wing at Offutt AFB, Nebraska, whose operatives can turn computer enhanced graphic output into hard facts on the Eastern Bloc's radar and missile defences. These 'sharp-end' based units are, of course, supported by a dozen others including, for example, the 9th Supply Squadron which has the tough job of stage-managing the

spares network worldwide. It also has to feed the aircraft one of three different types of fuel: JP-TS, JP-7 or JP-4.

Of all the aircraft on strength at Beale, the SR-71 places the severest strains on the support facilities. Around 20 of the original 32 airframes still exist, including the 'B' and 'C' specimens, but only ten 'A' models — excluding the follow-on test and evaluation machine at Palmdale — are usually active at any time. Typically, five will be at Beale for training, two at Mildenhall and up to three at Kadena. The remaining

Top:
SR-71B 64-17956 celebrated its 1,000th sortie with bold white markings on the belly and fins. This aircraft is the real workhorse of the 9th. *Lockheed*

Above centre:
SR-71A 64-17979 shows off its clean profile as it zooms over the runway threshold at Fairford in 1987. *John Dunnell*

Above:
SR-71A 64-17955 ends another sortie in a burst of brake 'chute at Norton AFB in November 1981. In strong crosswinds the 'chute would quickly be jettisoned to prevent it from weather-cocking into the tails. *Frank B. Mormillo*

Above:
U-2R 68-10340 stands parked at March AFB, California in October 1976. Note the lack of radar warning receivers on the wingtips, retro-fitted to all 'R' models in the late 1970s. TR-1s and U-2Rs wear different threat warning installations. *Frank B. Mormillo*

Below:
NASA's tasteful colours decorate their sole ER-2 (80-1063/N-706A) which is essentially a TR-1A without the military sensors. The aircraft's increased payload and performance have been welcomed by its users. *Jeff Puzzullo/AIR*

Bottom:
TR-1A 80-1074, just clear of Beale's runway, has the optical sensor fit in its Q-bay, one of the less common configurations. *Jeff Puzzullo/AIR*

airframes are rotated from storage and deep maintenance, as needed. Fortunately that need has not expanded markedly in recent years because it is already increasingly difficult to keep the aged Habus in peak condition. The 9th FMS's crew chiefs must often wish that Lockheed had been allowed to produce the three extra birds ('17982-84) cancelled from the original FY 1964 order: it is now 20 years since the last SR-71A left the Skunk Works' production shops. Many of the firms which supplied the original components are now defunct and the J58 engine is long out of production. Spares problems with widely-used front-line combat types in current mass production can be severe enough to necessitate cannibalisation on many an airfield, but with a limited-edition, hand-built rarity like the Habu the difficulties are obviously extreme. Progressive update programmes mean that newer, more reliable components can be introduced from other sources and this procedure is overseen by the SR-71 Advanced System Program Office (ASPO) at Norton AFB, California; also on the plus side, Kelly has claimed that each time an SR' goes trisonic it 'tempers' and toughens its airframe and that, theoretically, the Habu fleet could go on forever!

Even so, scarce J58 engines may still be on the shelf for up to a year awaiting parts. Invariably they go back to United Technologies/Pratt & Whitney at West Palm Beach, Florida, for 600-hour depot-level overhauls while SR-71 airframes are returned to Palmdale after three years for a complete strip-down. An increasing number of civilian field-service representatives from Lockheed and P&W work on the aircraft, and their experience is crucial. Keeping the highly complex J58 and its temperamental inlet/nozzle system, automatic engine trimming and chemical ignition systems on top line is an unusually demanding task by normal Air Force standards. Enlisted men on a four-year tour would have to spend half that time in special training to cope with the Habu's habits, hardly a cost-effective system. Maintenance man-hour figures for the aircraft and its powerplants therefore tend to be high — up to six weeks for an engine inspection, for example. The aircraft itself requires formidable supervision. Its airframe post-flight checklist alone runs to 650 items, reduced from 875 in earlier days; by comparison, the KC-135 has a mere seven! Even longer inspections are needed after 25hr and a major every 100hr. These will occupy about 10-12 full working days, with shifts. Engines are usually removed at 200hr, an operation which requires the outer wing sections to be swung upwards on hinges. A special dolly helps the five-man team to manoeuvre each J58 in and out of its close-fitting nacelle. Although the nacelle has a greater diameter than the fuselage, its contents run to extremely tight tolerances. An early problem in test flying was discovered when too rapid a descent from altitude caused the engine casing to cool faster than the compressor inside. Turbine blades actually rubbed against the cooler casing. A quick glance at the front of the SR-71 nacelle quickly shows the access problems. Anyone who has ever watched an RAF technician squeeze past the Airpass radar

Top and above left:
Some of the alloys used in SR-71A construction have a tensile strength of up to 200,000lb/sq in. The intake spikes have to withstand pressures of up to 14 tons at Mach 3. *Frank B. Mormillo*

Left:
From every angle the SR-71 looks sensational, especially the wide angle. *Frank B. Mormillo*

centrebody in a Lightning fighter's intake will not be surprised to hear that the SR's spike *and* engine have to come out for inspection and repair of the duct area. The aircraft spend a good deal of their time propped up on jacks too: tyres last for a mere 15 landings, at which point they are sent back to B. F. Goodrich to be recapped. Operating and maintenance costs are equivalent to those incurred in keeping two Wings of F-16s at combat-ready status!

Kelly Johnson's recollection that everything for the A-12 family structure had to be designed from scratch is felt particularly at the maintenance level. Normal cadmium-plated tools cause titanium corrosion, so special tool kits are required. An oil change means putting back the scarce, original oil only after it has been decontaminated by the manufacturer. Johnson, cost-conscious as ever, had the first $130/gal batch delivered in 1gal cans to reduce the chances of losing a whole batch! Habu alchemy also requires attention to the four hydraulic systems: A and B for flight control, L and R for utility subsystems and inlet control. Cooling these systems needs a heat exchange with the aircraft's internal fuel. The systems require special pumps, developed by Vickers Inc of Detroit. In the original test-rig, conventional pumps were operated in the system at the hot-and-high temperature of 550°F — and failed within an hour. Hydraulic fluid (specially developed, of course) must be kept oxygen-free to prevent coatings of burned deposit clogging up the valves. This requires the fluid to be constantly pressurised with nitrogen, in *or* out of the Habu. To test for hydraulic leaks, the fluid is run through a mobile 'hot cart' which brings it up to temperature. Technicians then feed the fluid back into the static Habu, watching for tiny puffs of blue smoke which would reveal leaks, but only at these high temperatures. Heat levels rule out standard O-ring seals too. These are metal or of fluorocarbon elastomeric material. A minute scratch or a tiny blockage by contaminant in the sealed areas can also be revealed with the 'hot smoke' test.

The special problems don't stop there. Silver-zinc batteries, pressurised with nitrogen to prevent explosion, have to be pulled out for a 48hr charge after each flight. Leaking JP-7 fuel, usually apparent beneath a standing Habu, tends to rot insulation or wiring and fluid lines, degrade paint and de-laminate the plastic honeycomb composite skins. Fuel tanks need resealing every 200hr. Items which would normally be greased are treated with a silicon-based lubricant instead. Screws and fasteners removed from the skin during maintenance have to be oven-baked before replacement so that they don't seize up in flight through differential expansion. Inadvertently punctured panels in the titanium skin areas have to be made-to-measure by Lockheed — there is no standard fit on these hand-made models. With such a demanding creature as their steed it is little wonder that SR-71 pilots are only guaranteed about three flights a month. (It is also tempting to become sceptical at the thought of a squadron of F-12B interceptors on QRA managing to rise to every intrusion by 'Bear' or 'Blinder'!)

Below:
John Dunnell's experienced camera-eye caught one of the most attractive of the 'Mildenhall fireball' photos when 64-17960 treated her 1986 audience to a 'wind-tunnel' aerodynamic vortex display and a large flaming mass of excess fuel. The weather at English air shows has a few advantages, perhaps.
John Dunnell

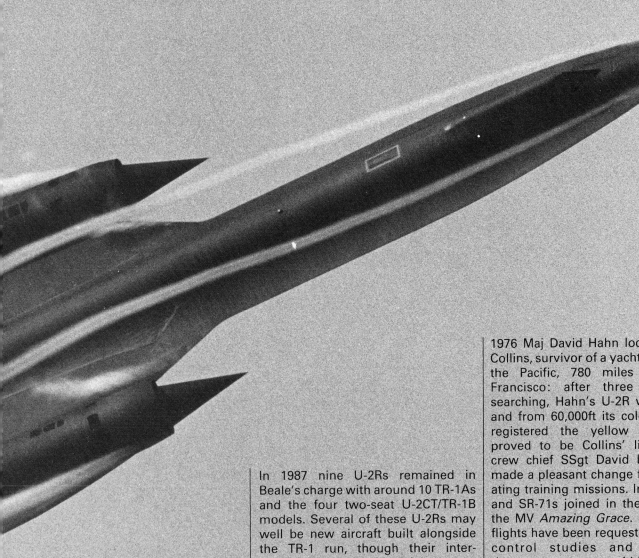

Black Angels

By comparison the TR-1 and U-2R pose far fewer headaches. Each aircraft normally has a crew chief and two airmen to tend it, with more specialised sensor functions covered by the 9th AMS. This crew will see each flight through to the point where the bird is pulled tail-first back into its 'barn', and then post-flight takes place. The Dragon is relatively simple and cheap to operate, and has a reliable airframe. With cruise fuel consumption of 160gal/hr and the ability to fly 'on the fumes' in the descent, she is obviously kinder on the taxpayer than the SR-71, whose fuel costs were estimated at £1,000/hr as far back as 1965!

Most Dragon flying at Beale is training, honing crews for the 95th RS or for U-2Rs flying from the 14th AD FOLs at Patrick AFB, Akrotiri or Osan.

In 1987 nine U-2Rs remained in Beale's charge with around 10 TR-1As and the four two-seat U-2CT/TR-1B models. Several of these U-2Rs may well be new aircraft built alongside the TR-1 run, though their interchangeable tails and serials are no help in establishing this. One of the TR-1Bs, usually 80-1065, is sent to Alconbury annually for around three weeks of check-rides for 95th RS crew. The U-2Rs are 'still actively engaged in imagery and Sigint collection on a worldwide basis, in support of strategic reconnaissance, crisis management and contigency operations', according to Beale. The extent to which their strategic role can interchange with the tactical mission of the TR-1 through sensor changes is a matter for speculation, but there are obviously strong possibilities here.

In its 12 years at Beale the 99th SRS has performed a wide variety of tasks, not all of them directly related to the strategic reconnaissance intelligence game. Just before their move to Beale, two surveillance flights over earthquake-stricken Guatemala were made at the request of the US Agency for International Development, for damage assessment. On 22 October

1976 Maj David Hahn located Bruce Collins, survivor of a yacht accident in the Pacific, 780 miles from San Francisco: after three weeks of searching, Hahn's U-2R was sent in and from 60,000ft its colour camera registered the yellow dot which proved to be Collins' life-raft. For crew chief SSgt David Leimbeck it made a pleasant change from generating training missions. In 1985 U-2s and SR-71s joined in the search for the MV *Amazing Grace*. Many other flights have been requested for flood control studies and hurricane damage-assessment within the USA.

U-2R surveillance of the Middle East pre-dated the Beale-based 9th SRW activities for several years. Two-to-three flights per day were made from RAF Akrotiri from August to December 1970, monitoring the cease-fire. Two aircraft remained at the base for four months and flights were suspended only after Egyptian objections. A repeat performance took place in 1973 to survey the Soviet build-up in Somalia. Tragically, surveillance for the 'Sinai Job' claimed a victim on 7 December 1977, when U-2R 68-10330 failed to lift off from Akrotiri, crashing into the base's Operations & Air Control Centre at 7am and exploding. Capt Robert A. Henderson, the 32-year-old pilot, died with four Cypriot base employees. The urgency of the mission caused a replacement aircraft (68-10340) to be sent via Mildenhall by 13 December. Three years later, on 6 February 1980, another Det 3 U-2R crashed, this time in the Black Sea in unknown circumstances. But the Akrotiri 9th SRW facility continues unabated, with 68-10332 almost certainly involved in Gulf surveillance off Iran at the time of writing.

Mildenhall's own Det 4 U-2R operations, code-named 'Senior Ruby', were the foundation of the present twin-SR-71 detachment. Occasional 99th SRS visits were made from 1976 onwards, the 68-10336 making daily flights after its arrival on 25 August. Aircraft tended to stay for irregular periods ranging from seven weeks (68-10339, the first Superpod-equipped visitor in 1978) to a few days (68-10333, brought over to help search for the MV *Muenchen*, missing off the Azores in December 1978); the longest stop-over was 130 days. Arrivals and departures were generally accompanied by KC-135 tankers to provide radio relay facilities. Det 4 officially began operations in 1979 with 68-10338 ('Snoopy') and -10339, staying for a year and 18 months respectively, up to June 1981. Elint, Comint and Sigint flights of up to 10hr duration were routine, many of them no doubt along WarPac borders. Brief detachments were also made to RAF Upper Heyford, where

68-10333 spent a month in 1973. Fulfilling the 'crisis management and contingency operations', part of the 99th SRS brief has involved Dragon drop-ins for jobs as varied as NATO exercise 'Teamwork 80' (68-10332), 'Northern Wedding' (68-10338), 'Reforger/Teamwork 76' (80-10336), and the crisis in Poland. The latter event brought Superpod-equipped '337 to Mildenhall to accompany '339. During its stay it sustained minor damage in a landing over-run, spending the night of 6 December 1982 in a field at RAF Alconbury. When it finally left on 22 February 1983 for Patrick AFB, it brought the regular U-2R Det 4 visits to an end. At about the same time a second SR-71A was added to Mildenhall's strength and TR-1 operations were commencing at Alconbury.

'Contingency operations' have regularly taken the black Dragons to

Below:
The 'other' TR-1B, 80-1064, displays its divided flaps, extended airbrakes and steep approach angle as it heads for Alconbury's runway. *David Mears*

other flashpoints too. Flying from Osan, South Korea, Det 2 aircraft regularly patrolled the border between the divided Koreas and allegedly peeped into the North from coastal orbits too. One of these aircraft stalled and crashed on take-off from Osan on 8 October 1984, resulting in a grounding order which kept the TR-1/U-2R fleet out of action for two months. Another 99th SRS U-2R took up temporary residence on the island of Diego Garcia in 1979 in response to the Iranian crisis and probably made extensive surveillance of the Gulf area. The loss of America's two listening posts in Iran after the revolution in that country brought Pentagon proposals in 1979 for the use of border-patrolling U-2Rs as a stop-gap measure for SALT-2 verification. The suggestion that the U-2Rs could intercept telemetry from the Tyuratam missile launch site smacked of 1959 rather than 1979, but it is possible that the Diego Garcia visit may have been connected.

The Grenada operation in 1983 brought a flurry of U-2R activity at Patrick AFB, the base for 9th SRW's Det 5. Its resident, 68-10338, was joined in October by '329 and '332

Above:
SR-71A 64-17980, seen here at Greenham Common, was one of the two Habus which took the post-strike photographs for Operation 'El Dorado Canyon', the attack on Libya in April 1986. *John Dunnell*

Right:
A little RAF Hawk led SR-71A 64-17980 to the 1983 Greenham Common International Air Tattoo. This unfortunate machine was daubed with graffiti by vandals during its stop-over for the show. *John Dunnell*

and all three studied the airfield under construction at Point Salines which the Reagan Administration insisted was intended for use by Cuban jet fighters. High altitude shots of this, and others showing 'Cuban housing', were released to the press as justification for Operation 'Stormfury', the invasion of Grenada. Other U-2Rs, flying direct from Beale, have been heavily involved in the Nicaraguan surveillance task. From 1982 onwards, Beale's U-2Rs have worked with other intelligence gatherers including 'Spruance' class destroyers. Some of President Reagan's 20% increase in his 1981 intelligence budget (a response to increased Soviet and Cuban influence in Central America) may have assisted in the restoration and expansion of the U-2R programme. Certainly, the U-2R has been a cost-effective eye on the day-to-day movements of the Sandinistas and other groups in El Salvador and Nicaragua. The appearance in 1979 of an entire, unsuspected Soviet combat brigade in Cuba was in itself sufficient to persuade the Congress that the U-2 was as valid then as in the 1950s. In the 1980s, restrictions on satellite operation following the suspension of Space Shuttle launches have once again underlined the need for effective back-up airborne intelligence-gathering systems.

Habu FOLs

Overseas deployment of the SR-71 began quite early in its career. The Vietnam whirlpool drew in all the available US reconnaissance media in the increasingly desperate attempt to identify precise targets which would have a telling, but politically

acceptable, effect on the course of the war. The 9th SRW's Det 1 at Kadena, Okinawa began intensive operations over the whole region in April 1968 although Agency A-12 flights from the same base undoubtedly provided vital data in the previous year too. The Habu's arrival coincided with the so-called bombing halt of 1968, when emphasis switched to interdicting the Ho Chi Minh Trail in Laos, and gave ample opportunity to study how North Vietnam was reconstructing its military machine after the three-year onslaught of 'Rolling Thunder'. It was also necessitated by the realisation that the U-2 was by then too vulnerable to be risked over the North's SAM sites. Habu performance and highly effective ECM enabled it to survive countless SAM launches and its current reputation as the 'most fired-at aircraft ever' (by SAMs, anyway) was well-founded in this period. Some idea of the intensity of SR-71 flying can be gained from the fact that high-time pilot Lt-Col Robert Powell has 400hr of South-East Asia 'combat' in his Habu log-book. At an average of five hours for each of these 'Giant Scale' missions, using four aircraft at a time for five years, there is obviously a good deal of interesting flying on record in the classified files. In November 1968 the 9th SRW received the Outstanding Unit Award for its South-East Asian flying. No combat losses were sustained and the Habu even managed to evade a Viet Cong sapper's attempt to blow up one of its number following an emergency four-day diversion to Udorn, Thailand, in 1972. Aircraft 64-17974, nicknamed 'Ichi Ban' after the 'Number One' designation of its squadron and detachment, and a play on the South-East Asian expression which means 'the best' (by contrast, 64-17975 carried the tail marking 'number 10' when its maintenance crews got fed up with it!), was allowed to accumulate at least 44 'snake' mission markings on its nose before the practice was discontinued. Sadly, there were two operational losses: 64-17969 after a double flame-out in appalling weather near Korat,

and 64-17978, a high-time combat veteran nicknamed 'Rapid Rabbit', which was decorated with Mr Hefner's infamous symbol of fecundity on its tails. Directed to return to Kadena despite pre-typhoon runway crosswinds rather than making a more prudent diversion, the aircraft departed the runway on a second landing attempt and ended up as spare parts.

Det 1's activities continued after the end of Vietnam hostilities with missions out of Kadena to observe the inexorable expansion of the North Vietnamese military effort, as seen from an off-shore track. Overflights of China were made regularly until President Nixon suspended them as part of his rapprochement with Peking in 1971. By that time there had been nearly 500 Chinese protests at US overflights! The emphasis then moved to Korea as Habus collaborated with the Osan-based U-2R detachment in observing the fragile peace-line. As part of North Korea's propaganda war, repeated accusations of SR-71 overflights and air-space violations have been made since 1980. Their frustration finally persuaded the North Koreans to take a SAM-2 shot at one of these flights, using the Chokta-ri missile base, in August 1981. Acrimonious governmental exchanges resulted but the 'imperialistic aggressors' flights have continued unscathed.

North Korea has been by no means alone in voicing its unintended tributes to the Blackbirds' all-seeing eye through protests at its 'provocative acts of espionage'. Cuba has also been a regular subject for the cameras. In 1978 an aircraft from Beale was sent to determine whether the MiG-23 fighters which a satellite had detected on the island were nuclear-capable or not. In the event, they were revealed on the photos as relatively harmless, but 'Giant Plate' flights around Cuba's airspace have gone on. The supposed Cuban influence in Central American areas of US interest has put the 'notorious Blackbird' on the front pages of newspapers throughout the region. A mythical consignment of Soviet MiGs which was thought to have arrived in Nicaragua turned out to be Soviet Mi-8 helicopters instead when seen through the Habu's eye. Wider circuits from Beale may well have taken in drug-growing areas of South America from 1975 as part of the US government's anti-narcotics drive.

Mildenhall, Suffolk, has sheltered one of the liveliest Blackbirds' nests.

Det 4 began to accommodate short-stay 1st SRS visitors alongside its regular 99th SRS U-2R from 1976 onwards. SR-71A 64-17972 (the most frequent UK visitor) turned up with two C-141s loaded with support gear on 20 April and although it flew only twice, its 10-day TDY was the first of 33 visits by 12 aircraft up to August 1987. In fact Mildenhall's very first visitation was for the Atlantic record-breaking effort (Exercise 'Glowing Speed') by 64-17972 in September 1974. Maj James Sullivan with RSO Maj Noel Widdifield flew 'Aspen 01' (all Beale SR-71A training flights have 'Aspen' call-signs) from Beale to a New York time-gate and from there to a very public landing at Farnborough Air Show, having reached the London time-gate in 1hr 54min 56.4sec. The return trip to Los Angeles from Mildenhall on 13 September set another record time. Lockheed took a full-page advert in the *Times* to broadcast the event, but there was little need — the SR-71A was a star already. Rather more permanent arrangements were made in 1980 when the first of two purpose-built hangars was installed at Mildenhall, complete with piped air for engine starts rather than the twin V8 600hp Buick racing car motor-start method used previously. From then on, the 9th's visits of 10-14 days in the 1970s were increased to a couple of months apiece and eventually to periods in excess of a year, depending on serviceability. Some have lasted longer than others: 64-17980 had a very brief stay in early 1982 due to mechanical problems and had to be replaced by '974, the former 'Ichi Ban'. On its return to the UK, '980 was further insulted by being daubed with paint by peace protestors after a charity fund-raising airshow, ironically, with almost para-military precision; there were some much more sinister shark-mouthed fighters to be found at Greenham Common that night, but the unarmed Habu's matt black finish presented itself as a handy blackboard for the vandals. SR-71A 64-17962, also, had but a brief stay — only one sortie prior to its July 1983 return to Beale. Habu crews normally go on TDY for six weeks, alternating Detachments, with about eight weeks at Beale between trips; though length and frequency does vary with crew availability and demands from higher authority.

Increases in SR-71 utilisation at Det 4 were made gently, with due deference to UK sensitivity on the spyplane issue. However, in April

1982 it was announced that a 12% increase in reconnaissance funding, together with special permission from HM Government, would enable a second Habu to join the Mildenhall roster. Accordingly, a second hangar was erected and both sheds came into use after '962 christened them in August 1985. As at Beale, aircraft now tend to keep their own hangars. In early 1987, '960 occupied the left shed (nearest the runway) and '973 the right. A purpose-built detuner was installed in May 1980 to reduce the day-and-night thunder of J58 ground-tests for the long-suffering locals.

There has been plenty of trade for the double-Det since its inception. Peak activity has centred on various 'contingency operations'. SR-71A '974 flew daily missions to check on a large Soviet Fleet exercise in April 1984. Operation 'El Dorado Canyon', the strike against Libya, saw both birds airborne in the early morning on 15 and 16/17 April 1986. This time, '980 was on top form and with '960 it used its OBC camera-nose to obtain effective post-strike photos of the 48th TFW and USN attack aircrafts' results, backing up the latter's video-taped TRAM and Pave Tack FLIR imagery with top-quality glossies. Supplementing the six to eight KC-135Q tankers normally at Mildenhall on TDY were two KC-10As, in use

Top left:
U-2R 68-10332 and SR-71A 64-17964 in company at March AFB's open day in 1979. *Frank B. Mormillo*

Centre left:
SR-71A 64-17977 was written off after aborting its take-off on 10 October 1968. Maj Gabriel A. Kardong and RSO Maj James A. Kogler got out OK, but the aircraft was scrapped. *Appeal Democrat*

Bottom left:
The second SR-71B to be built, 64-17957, crashed on approach to Beale on 11 January 1968. Lt-Col Robert A. Sowers and student Capt David E. Fruehauf got out in one piece.
Appeal Democrat

Above:
Maj James W. Hudson lost his life in an unsuccessful ejection on 23 March 1971; instructor Lt-Col Jack R. Thornton stayed with the aircraft until it had slid to a halt, and stepped out. *Appeal Democrat*

for the first time on SR-71A operations. The twin Habu sorties may have been flown to provide an air-spare in view of the urgency of the mission. The technique was used once again in August 1987, as the Gulf tanker war drew in US Navy escort involvement. Two missions were flown, on 28 August and the normally-embargoed Sunday morning following, using 64-17964 and -17980, once again OBC-nose-

equipped for snap-shot work. Two KC-10As and three KC-135Qs were launched to support a lengthy flight by one of the pair, the other Habu returning after a briefer time, possibly as air-spare. It is difficult to believe that the flight did not take in large areas of the Iran-Iraq battlefront.

Mildenhall's SR-71s have enjoyed an excellent safety record and their glamorous public profile has been enhanced by several airshow appearances since 1977. Some of those given at Mildenhall itself have demonstrated the fiery character of the machine to its full, though the rather exuberant fighter-type aerobatics at the 1987 Air Fete resulted in an overstressed Blackbird returning to Palmdale for repairs. However, there is never any doubt that the SR-71 is as serious as it looks. Flights along the East German and Czech borders, or a Baltic circuit taking in coastal areas of Poland and the USSR, give NATO the chance to look deep into those areas. The Habu can operate over these distances without using the FOL sites if necessary, as the 10 flights from Griffiss AFB, New York, over the Middle East during the 1973 Yom Kippur War demonstrated. However, the tanking requirement is formidable and the 9th SRW will obviously diserse its operations from Beale as long as it can.

5
Habu

Operational missions flown by the Beale Habus and their TDY colleagues at Det 4 in England and Det 1 in Okinawa, Japan, are broadly similar in their objective: as Beale put it, 'to glean intelligence in response to the Peacetime Aerial Reconnaissance Program', or PARPRO for short. This usually calls for a stand-off, peripheral recce flight along a border, as directed by the National Command Authorities and JCS. (In wartime, or times of tension, missions make greater use of Habu's penetrative capability, in accordance with Emergency War order provisions drawn up in Washington.)

Mission planning begins anything up to two days before the flight. The numbers of staff and groundcrew associated with a fully-fledged operational mission demand more talent and man-hour input than any other aircraft in the West's inventory. Routes embracing up to 16 waypoints (recent digital avionics updates may have extended this) are drawn on the map — the 'black line' — and fed into the operations room computer which in turn furnishes the mission tapes to be loaded into the Habu's Northrop Astro-Inertial Navigation System (AINS) up to 24 hours before launch, powered by a pacemaker which

keeps the systems ticking over a dormant, standby posture, ready for the mission the next day, *or* night. The 415lb/sq in nitrogen-inflated 22-ply tyres are checked, as are the neatly-packed drag 'chute, miles of hydraulics, and tons of avionics and payloads, via built-in test equipment and scrupulous visual inspection. Some 2½ hours before the scheduled take-off time, payload specialists will make final checks on the aircraft, followed by elements of the Physiological Support Division (PSD) who will ensure that the onboard LOX and other life-support systems are satisfactory.

The aircrew review the route and study film imagery and maps several hours in advance of the mission, receiving briefings on weather and mission objectives and familiarising themselves with the key waypoints which the RSO will later monitor on the map and digital drift sight displays in the rear cockpit. The mission is ingrained into the pilot's memory too, as he psychs himself up for the precision flying ahead; everything, including tanker rendezvous and waypoint co-ordinates, ascent, mission altitude and descent curves, engine settings and temperatures, speeds and even bank angles, are pre-planned down to individual knots, degrees, minutes and seconds — a rigid — or as US pilots describe any restricted mode of flying, 'canned' — mission profile in extreme. The pilot knows that he must stick to his plan to the letter if he is to keep his RSO — and their bosses — happy. The crew must also familiarise themselves with emergency fields along each leg of the loop, as the flight-plan is known: it takes 200 miles to descend from trisonic flight, and the procedures must be followed precisely even in acute emergencies, so meticulous attention to detail is a prerequisite. For important missions, this homework is studied by a

back-up crew. The teams stick together as two-man affairs and if one of them is not feeling medically 'up to stuff' both men may stand down and let the substitute team step in. For top priority missions, two Blackbirds may be launched, with one ready to be substituted in the event the primary bird is forced to abort.

Three hours prior to launch the crew report to the PSD for some 'low residue' chow: steak and scrambled eggs. With an average of three-to-five hours in the suit to follow, depending on the nature of the impending sortie, beans and chillis are definitely out! A thorough pre-flight medical ensues. Passed fit, suiting-up follows, about 75 minutes prior to take-off. This is carried out by approximately five suit specialists who dress their 'knights' in the PSD, located adjacent to the flight-line. (The 100-strong PSD organisation is drawn from Beale's hospital, 20-30 of whose personnel are on rotational TDY at U-2R and SR-71 FOLs at any one time.) The S1030 'gold suit', introduced in 1977, is a cumbersome, multi-layered garment which consumes 20-30 minutes of time to fit and check; it is mandatory for all flights above 45,000ft — ie all SR-71 sorties — and is sealed in the shop with helmet, boots and gloves clipped in place.

At this stage the adrenalin starts to build up. Dan House recalled one of his recent missions: 'My RSO and I were selected to fly a search and rescue (SAR) mission in the SR-71. We were both excited by the prospects of this for several reasons. First, and foremost, the thought of helping save a fellow human being lost at sea appealed to the humanitarian part of us. Second, it would have been a challenge professionally to properly fly the mission. And third, it would have meant more flying time (more fun) for us.

'The plan was to take-off from Beale, refuel just west of San Francisco, fly to Hawaii, refuel again, search a 100×400-mile rectangle 300 miles west of Hawaii, descend and refuel over Hawaii again, then fly home to California. This was to take about six hours. We planned for an entire day, trying to cover every conceivable contingency as best we could with the time and information available.

'On the day of the flight, we filed our flight plan and talked to our first tanker crew before going to PSD for pre-flight meal and suit-up. As we ate, we noticed that everyone in the building was excited about the flight and I'll admit that we were also. Meal finished, maintenance forms checked with the crew chief who brought

Above:
A Habu taxies from Beale's 'barns' to the 'hammerhead', preparatory to a mission. Today, SR-71s carry only minute red serial numbers on their fins, a practice introduced on the U-2 20 years previously, and a sharp contrast to the bold US Air Force and serial number logos carried as standard until 1983. Lockheed photo by Eric Schulzinger

them to us, then the routine preflight physical. We both had slightly elevated pulse and blood pressure but that was to be expected. We almost ran to the dressing room where our technicians were waiting to assist us in putting on the full pressure suits.

'Things were going smoothly until someone came in and told me I had a phone call. I thought this was a bit unusual as I walked to the phone, but maybe they had some new information that would be of assistance to us. I picked up the phone.

' "Major House."

' "Hi, Dan. This is John in scheduling. You're not going to believe this, but . . ."

' "But what?" I said.

' "But . . . they just called from Hawaii. They found the guy you were going to look for. Your flight is cancelled."

'Realising I'd lost a flight and a chance to be a hero, I said, "John, if they're still on the line, tell them to throw him back in the water!" '

All going according to plan with 45min left before lift-off, the crew climb into the PSD van, to be driven to their aircraft, their suits connected to on-board air-conditioning systems. The boarding steps will be in place for the whole ensemble arriving in the van, ready for the PSD to help the crew into the cockpit on signal from the ground support personnel. With pilot and RSO suitably connected to on-board oxygen at 2lb/sq in, and firmly lap-, heel- and shoulder-buckled in their Lockheed SR-1 ejection seats, the PSD retreat from the hangar — though elements will remain on constant 24-hour call near the hyperbaric facility in case the crew later suffer a decompression emergency and need urgent treatment to avoid the potentially lethal hazards of untreated CO poisoning, air embolisms or gas gangrene associated with the bends. The full pressure suits are not worn

Below:
Tails and nosegear move in unison as the pilot applies right rudder to steer the bird along the taxi ramp at Greenham Common in 1985. The pedal-operated rudders provide yaw stability during unstart, engine failures on take-off and compensation for cross-winds. The trailing-edge elevons provide pitch and roll control, with the outboard elevons rigged 3° trailing edge 'up' relative to the inboard surfaces, to reduce root bending moments at high speeds. They are slaved together via a torque tube system which runs across the nacelle. Stick movements are converted into elevon pitch and roll commands via an elevon 'mixer' in the Habu's boat-tail. *John Dunnell*

for the macho image! Pre-breathing oxygen to purge the body of nitrogen follows during the ensuing pre-take-off routine and ascent at lower altitudes, for a total of about 55 minutes.

Settled in the cockpit with hatches still open, the crew first go through the pre-flight motions — test checks of the avionics and switch settings, things that are checked umpteen times to ensure a successful mission. Half an hour before take-off, engine start is the first move towards independence. The normally viscous engine oil will have been pre-heated to 86°F to enable the turbines to be started up, which, at cooler, forward bases such as Mildenhall, may have taken up to 3½ hours on a cold winter morning. An air drive unit coupled to both nacelles is used to spool the J58s up to a screaming 3,200rpm, engaged from the starting system built into the hangars. When correct rpm is reached the pilot advances the first throttle from cut-off to idle, which automatically squirts Tri-Ethyl Borane (TEB) into the spinning system to ignite the low volatility JP-7/LF-2A; with a positive start, signified by an electric-green flash in the free-floating nozzles, the procedure is repeated with the other powerplant, at which point the ser-

vice lines are unclipped from both engines. Pre-taxi checks consume a further quarter-of-an-hour as the hydraulics are cycled and the flight control surfaces flexed. With the heavy metal canopies clanked shut and secured and a final thumbs-up from the crew chief floor-managing the show, the boarding steps are wheeled away and the growling SR-71A becomes a completely self-contained matt black capsule of men, sensors and fuel, dripping JP-7 from its cool, loosely-fitting wet delta. With all systems 'go' the pilot advances the throttles up from idle to push the pointy end of the SR' out of the 'barn'. Nosewheel steering and the huge rudders move in sympathy as the bird executes a 90° turn on to the taxiway, rambling along to the pre-take-off hold — the 'hammerhead' — with brake checks while on the move. Wheels are chocked again at this stage so that the J58s can be revved up to full military power to permit exhaust gas temperature (EGT) to be monitored and throttle settings trimmed accordingly — differential thrust could cause more than a minor nuisance later on. Auto trim is then engaged and takes charge of symmetry.

The heat is on! With clearance to roll from air traffic control (ATC), the awesome organ-like suction from the intakes echoes around the base as the crew await the scheduled take-off time with considerable anticipation. The on-board AINS will already be plotting position based on 52 stars stored in its memory, cued by the RSO to take constant sextant shots from its flush glass peephole just aft of the rear cockpit, to keep the inertial platform aligned correctly throughout the mission. Following the 'okay' from the support crew (who amble down the runway in two pick-up trucks to ensure minimum risk of FOD ingestion) and watched by the back-up Habu crew in the 'mobile control' vehicle, at the pre-planned launch time the pilot advances the throttles to initial afterburner position. The warmed-up J58s respond quickly. With a positive 'burn' light shining on the console the twin levers are pushed to maximum power. At 120,000lb, the partly-fuelled bird lunges forward unexpectedly fast as the 'ka-boom' of the 'burners punch it forward, leaving a cloud of unspent gas in its wake. Calling for the afterburners is akin to pulling the 'go' handle on a roller-

coaster and pilots are relatively passive at this stage. As Maj Burk once remarked: 'On take-off the whole airplane is trembling. The afterburners rarely light together, and we're 107ft forward of the monsters. At that point I feel I'm merely a passenger; I'm just aiming it down the runway.' Maj Dan House added: 'What gets one's attention in the front cockpit is that the afterburners seldom light at the same time. Since the engines are quite far apart, this causes an asymmetric thrust that pushes the nose of the plane toward the side of the runway. If the pilot puts in a rudder correction to straighten the plane, he can be assured that the other afterburner will decide to light at the same time, compounding the correction and pushing the nose toward the other side of the runway!' Speed builds up at a dramatic pace. Seconds later, with 180kt on the indicator, the pilot hauls gently back on the stick, rotating the Habu up to 12° pitch, unsticking the bird at 210kt, 4,000ft down the ramp, its fleeting departure marked by thunder and the tell-tale orange shock diamonds shooting out of the variable jet nozzles. The gear is tucked up as soon as possible to avoid over-stressing the sturdy but 300kt airspeed-limited legs. Exceeded, and the crew may well have to make do with a belly landing on a foamy runway on their return; but Kelly Johnson and his team-mates are proud of the fact that no Blackbird has ever suffered a critical leg failure. Climb at the initial 10° pitch pulls the ½-⅔ fuel-laden Habu up at 10,000ft p m.

The three-axis, triple-redundant Honeywell Stability Augmentation System (SAS) is engaged shortly after take-off to dampen pitch, roll and yaw instabilities, in true control-configured vehicle mode. The SR' is anything but an unfeathered arrow, but does possess some inherent instability which must be checked, especially as trim requirements change with speed and height. The SAS will remain engaged whether the Blackbird is being flown by hand or autopilot. With the pilot in authority of the aircraft, surface limiters cut in to prevent him overcontrolling the sensitive machine, physically limiting manual stick roll elevon inputs and imposing rudder yaw limits via the tail's hydraulic actuators. (The canted tails are limited to 20° left or right rudder below Mach 0·5; 10° either way above that speed. Pitch control is limited to 24° 'up' elevon, and 11° down; roll control is limited to ±14° deflection above Mach 0·5, and ±24° below that speed.)

Only 2½ or so minutes into the flight, the pilot retards the throttles to just under maximum military power, trimmed for Mach 0·9 cruise at the 'magic' 26,000ft (FL 260), where everything stops for a drink. Already the Blackbird's skin will have begun to warm, expand and seal, ready for a fuel top-up. Typically, the KC-135Q tanker and SR-71 will approach head-on, assisted by TACAN (tactical air navigation) outputs from the 'Q'-bird. At 20 miles to go the tanker turns on to a reciprocal heading ready for the Blackbird to join up behind — unlike fighters, which have to juggle into position 'off the wing', up behind the go-juice donor, the Habu handler can leave most of the preparatory jinking to the Stratotanker. Contrails in a wet sky or a squirt of juice from the tanker's boom assists visual contact. The plug at 350kt (375kt with the re-engined KC-135R) is relatively straightforward, but there the simplicity ends. The tanker is going fast and the Habu slow to maintain the union, and as 60,000lb of fuel is transferred at a steady 5,500lb/min — wings first, then fuselage tanks — the balancing act gets reversed as the tanker offloads weight into its svelte client. The SR-71 driver will usually add a

Above:
SR-71 64-17955, carrying the ADP's famous insignia and nicknamed 'The Flower' (a derisive play on the well known 'fragrant' attributes of the skunk), receives a fuel top-up from KC-135Q 58-0112, assigned to the — then — 100th ARW. A 'Q'-bird will take off and orbit on station prior to each Habu launch, ready to replenish the thirsty Mach 3+ jet as it pops through the clouds en route to the stratosphere. *Lockheed*

little left afterburner to keep pace, which has the added bonus of yawing the beast to the right, providing a forward view unobscured by the centre frame. Another reason for this asymmetric manoeuvre is that Lockheed only fitted a de-icer to the left windshield, and the drinking is never done without visual contact; those bright lights on the tanker's belly must always be kept in view, lest disaster occurs. (Aircraft 64-17970 was lost in this fashion on 17 June 1970 when it struck its tanker over Texas. Thankfully, both SR' crew members ejected successfully and

the rugged KC' plus crew arrived home in one piece, albeit with a badly bent tail.) Radio silence is maintained via the intercom, active when the two birds are physically joined via the flying boom.

Following the top-up a quarter-of-an-hour on, the birds break and the SR-71 is hauled gently up to FL 330 at 10ft/sec, ready for the famous 'Dipsy Doodle' dive back down to FL 280 to help the beast accelerate through the sound barrier. Acceleration to supersonic speeds can be accomplished quite easily in level flight, but first, it's better to get the 'hell out', and second, the Habu is a real gas-guzzler at transonic speeds, so a fast transition equates with less of the valuable fuel burnt up in the process.

Manhandled, SAS-assisted flight is replaced by the autopilot as the machine climbs in afterburner and pulls through 510kt. Trim input is minimal; the chines make up 40% of the lift and compensate for this shift in centre of pressure as the big delta prods the sound barrier. Transition to higher Mach numbers presents a whole new set of demands on the pilot, who must orchestrate the inlet, engine and bypass doors as the machine becomes a turbo-ramjet. This is a purely automatic function performed by the Honeywell Digital Automatic Flight Inlet Control System (DAFICS). First introduced on a trials basis in 1981, DAFICS manages the inlet and control systems to ensure correct airflow at any given speed, but in a worst-case situation the pilot must be prepared to handle a systems failure and manually adjust the systems via selector switches, prior

to a possible abort. In all cases, instrument scanning is necessary to ensure correct operation. As airspeed builds up, airflow is increasingly, bypassed to the aft end of the nacelle for ramjet operation. Lockheed engineers Kelly Johnson and Ben Rich have always enjoyed having a poke at P&W's chief designer William H. Brown and his colleagues, reminding them that as speed reaches Mach 3+, the big, gutsy J58s provide as little as 17·6% of the thrust! — though in all fairness they are willing to concede that their bird wouldn't even get airborne without the 65,000lb of total thrust developed by the J58s in afterburner mode at sea level. DAFICS is triple-redundant so it's usually a case of the pilot watching the instruments to confirm that all is going well. Auto-inlet or start operation begins to function at between Machs 1·6 and 1·7. Spike centrebody movement via hydraulic rams is monitored on the cockpit display; at Mach 3·2, they assume a retracted posture 26in aft, maintaining the shockwave at the inlet throat. The suction from the inlets makes up some 54% of the thrust — 'with all running smoothly, the bird sort of sucks its way through the sky', as one pilot put it.

DAFICS also compensates for the dreaded unstart phenomenon, when the shockwave pops out of the inlet turning tons of thrust into tons of drag on one wing and creating a momentary violent yaw before corrective action is initiated. Originally corrected by the inlet automatic restart system (IARS), unstart could and can be an unpleasant experience

J58 Air Flow Patterns
Static aircraft at top; high-speed at bottom.

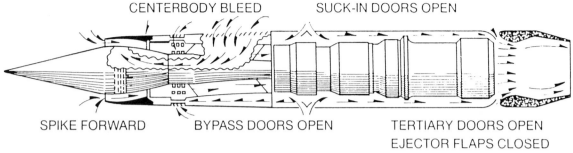

CENTERBODY BLEED   SUCK-IN DOORS OPEN

SPIKE FORWARD   BYPASS DOORS OPEN   TERTIARY DOORS OPEN
EJECTOR FLAPS CLOSED

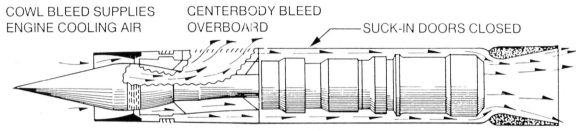

COWL BLEED SUPPLIES   CENTERBODY BLEED
ENGINE COOLING AIR   OVERBOARD   SUCK-IN DOORS CLOSED

SPIKE IN AFT DESIGN   BYPASS DOORS CLOSED   TERTIARY DOORS CLOSED
POSITION. IF INLET   ON STANDARD DAY—   EXTERNAL EJECTOR
SHOULD UNSTART SPIKE   OPEN AS REQUIRED   FLAPS FULL OPEN
MOVES FORWARD TO   TO POSITION SHOCK
RESTART THE INLET   OR RESTART INLET

despite the spontaneity of the auto restart system.

Dan House explained the procedures: 'The inlets are the heart of the propulsion system. They consist of movable spikes to control the shock wave, and bypass doors to control pressure. When things are not quite in balance the inlet doors will "talk" to you. If they are bouncing off the stops, the limits of travel, they generate a rumbling sound remotely similar to propellers being out of synchronisation. When this happens, the pilot can try to eliminate the sound by adjusting the doors manually, or he can elect to sit it out and hope the sound goes away. Sometimes, this will result in an "unstart". Since the inlet can be producing more than half of your usable thrust, this can cause a considerable yawing moment. Depending on altitude, attitude, speed and power setting, this can be quite gentle — or violent enough to bounce your helmet off the canopy!' Old stories of Habu handlers dismounting with cracked visors are not based on myth.

'After the initial head-banging we have definite procedures to follow which include maintaining positive aircraft control, monitoring the automatic restart function, and checking the affected engine for proper indications — EGT, nozzle position, fuel flow, rpm. We will also check appro-priate hydraulic systems and electrical systems, including numerous circuit breakers. If the automatic restart system doesn't work, or if the unstart continues, we take control of the inlet manually. When this happens on one side, the pilot's workload increases by 50%. Double manual inlets will double the pilot's overall cockpit workload. These figures are approximate and are strictly my opinion. Inlet parameters vary with speed, altitude, outside air temp, AOA, and sideslip, which requires manual control to be conservative, therefore less efficient than automatic, thus increasing fuel consumption. The only thing worse than a manual inlet is no inlet at all, because no control of the inlet means you stay in subsonic configuration.'

The pilot is constantly monitoring the EGT gauge to ensure correct operating temperatures lest an unstarted engine continue to ingest a rich fuel-only intake and burn itself out. Other things to be kept in check as the pilot sits with his arms folded but rapidly eyeballing the instruments is the fuel transfer system. As Mach 3 is approached, the auto fuel transfer system will pump fuel aft to move the centre of gravity backwards. The Air Data Computer furnishes knots equivalent airspeed (KEAS), altitude and Mach numbers in digits on the Triple Display Indicator to assist the pilot in assimilating the larger number of critical read-outs; over the intercom, he will seek reassurance from the RSO regarding heading, AINS status, and timing — are they on schedule?

'Going Tactical'
At FL 600 the RSO switches off the ATC identification friend or foe (IFF) squawk box. The Habu is flying a classified route from now on and its presence is kept as a well-hidden secret. The USAF claims the bird can fly 'above 80,000ft' and Capt Robert C. Helt and his RSO Maj Larry A. Elliot set the published record in Bicentennial year of a sustained cruise at 85,068·9ft; with a good mission payload, FL 830 is a fair estimate of operational cruise altitude, which can increase slightly as more fuel is guzzled (at a rate of, according to a 1964 statement by Maj Gen John D. Laralle, 8,000 USgal/hr. The Attitude Director Indicator's (ADI's) Instrument Landing System (ILS) 'pitch steering bar' serves as a guide to inertial vertical velocity; when the bar is aligned with the miniature aircraft symbol the Habu is holding steady at cruise height.

From the rapidly heating back seat, the RSO is monitoring the way the mission tape is running the show, via the AINS. Although the system can be manually updated by the RSO — and he can, in effect, fly the aircraft in the horizontal plane from the otherwise

controlless nav-office by commanding 'direct steer' back home or to the next waypoint, at the push of a button, the package is quintessentially an automatic chauffeur or, as Kelly describes it, 'a take me home James' system. All the same, the AINS is not infallible and the RSO's attention is absorbed with navigation as a primary task. He monitors the AINS 'control head course error window', which provides read-outs on current position and drift in digits, to within a tenth of a mile. Similar information is presented in less

Left:
SR-71 64-17972 in its anonymous all-black decor cruising at lower altitude. From 83,000ft the Habu can cover 'over 100,000 sq miles of territory an hour' according to the USAF, using cameras, radar and Elint sensors. *Lockheed*

Below:
A dazzling into-the-sun shot of SR-71A 64-17955 getting into the groove for a fuel top-up from one of SAC's new re-engined KC-135R Stratotankers. The aircraft will contact at 375kt.
Boeing Military Airplane Co

comprehensive form on the pilot's ADI, via a course deviation bar. If the bird strays from the black line the pilot can override the autopilot by pressing the stick 'disconnect steering' button and then employ stick and rudder, très gentilement, within the control-configured restraints imposed by the limiters to steer the Habu back on course. From both crewmen's point of view, straying from the black line can be serious, resulting in anything from embarrassment to a major international scandal. Travelling at 3,100ft/sec in the fast lane demands constant attention. Lt-Col Albert N. Pennington, the first SR-71 RSO to qualify in the USAF, summed it up long ago when he said 'we have to be totally aware of where we are at any given moment, especially when we cover 30 miles every minute'. In the unlikely event the AINS goes screwball, it's a case of all hands to the maps and flight-plans and providing the pilot with manual instructions — fast! AINS reliability is 99%+, and typically the AINS control head will flash up a series of 'on-track zeroes', signifying that all is well.

More likely, it is a matter of monitoring the radar warning display and switching on the music — the electronic countermeasures — as sharp red sticks and stones are lobbed skyward. Habus have featured as targets even during stand-off PARPRO missions, and it is a *deadly* serious business. The potential threats embrace SAMs and MiGs (AAA does not figure into the equation at 83,000ft), some of which are capable of smacking or peppering an unwary Habu. Of the SAMs, the well-established, mature SA-5 is one of the most lethal. NATO codenamed 'Gammon', this SAM is a 54ft-long projectile, of which 1,200-1,500 serve with the USSR's ZA-PVO (the strategic home defence missile forces). Ground-based surveillance and height-finder radars put the weapon on course, after which time the SAM's own 2ft active radar dish locks and homes in on the target. Range is around 155 miles and ceiling well in excess of a Blackbird. Obviously, the trick is to fox the surveillance radar, so that the missiles waste valuable rocket fuel chasing ghosts. 'Range gate stealing' modes are employed by the RSO's box of tricks to generate spurious range and height inputs by providing false echoes out of time-step with the true returns, along with amplitude- or frequency-modulated jamming to provide false azimuth and heading. Activation of the ECM is very much at the RSO's discretion (mis-management of ECM could actually cause position to be given away), the desired effect being to watch SAMs pop off way off mark like distant fireworks, as some ineffectual pyrotechnic display shot up purely for in-flight crew entertainment.

The success of the Habu's jamming equipment has become legend in SAC, and in September 1979 *Aviation Week & Space Technology* reported that up to 1977, when President Carter suspended the Cuban over-flights (10 days after taking up office), the 9th SRW Mach 3 community had drawn no fewer than 810 SAMs! A high proportion were encountered during flights over North Vietnam, along the borders of North Korea, and the Middle East, but none have found their mark. But it's not just ECM that has enabled the fleet to maintain its integrity; the SR-71's stealth structure contributes a great deal too. The canted, vertical stabilisers and wedge-like, signal-trapping characteristics of the delta — over 20% of the Habu's skin is high-strength, radar-transparent plastic — and virtually negligible head-on radar cross-section make the Habu a very difficult target to acquire indeed. That was the ADP men's goal when they first put pen to paper and got out their slide rules. And they did a fine job.

MiGs, perhaps, present a bigger threat, and are far more likely to rattle the SR's tail. Elements of the Soviet's home air defence force are forward-deployed in times of peace speci-

fically to deter incursions by US reconnaissance aircraft. Defecting 'Foxbat' pilot Lt Victor Ivanovich Belenko, who 'crash-landed' his Mach 3 dash-capable MiG-25 at Hakodate, Japan, on 6 September 1976, told US officials that his 14-strong 'Foxbat' outfit located at Sakharovka had but one primary function: 'to check photography over Vladivostok by the two-to-three SR-71s the US has based on Okinawa'. Similar units are based near the Baltic in the northwest, along the East German border, and adjacent to the Black Sea. Belenko, apparently, exhibited the same colourful style as American fighter pilots and is said to have a penchant for salty language and bravado, revealing to his CIA debriefers that he had had 'an ambition to shoot down an SR-71 reconnaissance plane'. Fighter and air intercept missile technology has

progressed in leaps and bounds since 1976, and, while the Soviets do make the occasional mistake — witness the tragic downing of a Korean Air Lines 747, probably mistaken for a USAF RC-135 'Ferret' — Habu backseaters ensure the bird stays firmly on the black line, out of bounds to ambitious fighter pilots. With all Soviet interceptors able to employ long-range infrared-homing weapons, the big white-hot Habu nozzles cry out 'come and get me' to every infra-red search and

track system within range, so any penetration of 'Foxbat'- or 'Foxhound'-studded skies will require considerable nerve and effective GCI radar-jamming, to keep the fuel-limited fighters guessing; but cruising at Mach 3·2 at a nose-up attitude of 15°, the Habu could be said to be mocking its potential predators!

The mission tape is also responsible for cueing the sensor payload over target. The Habu's recon suite can cover 100,000sq miles of territory

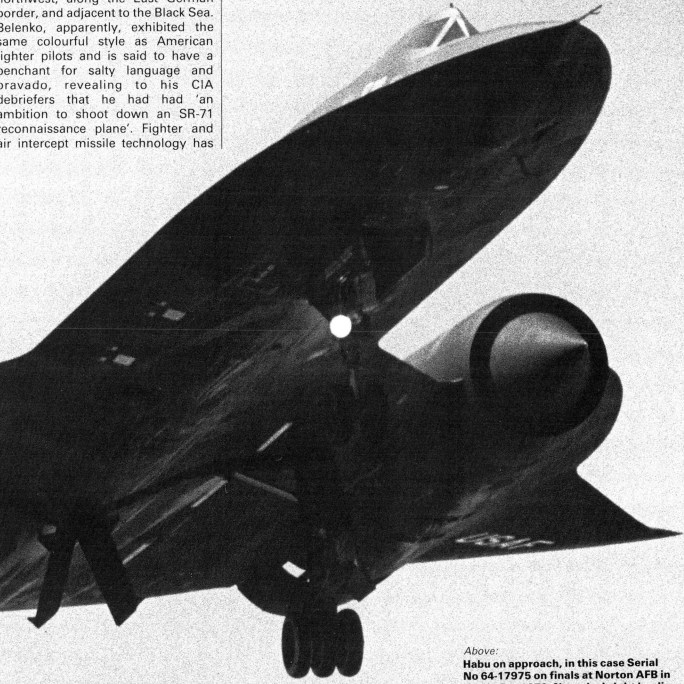

Above:
Habu on approach, in this case Serial No 64-17975 on finals at Norton AFB in November 1979. Note the bright landing light on the nosegear leg, and the white stencil data under the fuselage. The white stripes denote the hoist points under the delta; the smaller markings under the forward fuselage and chines are related with the sensor doors, hoist points, and fuel and access panels.
Frank B. Mormillo

an hour, using a variety of vertical and oblique cameras and SLARs for panoramic horizon-to-horizon and sideways-looking operation, generating a massive backlog of work for the intelligence community. The target whizzes by fairly fast at Mach 3, and post-mission it is usually a case of all 9th RTS eyes and ears to the celluloid and magnetic tape and junking all but the vital patches, which receive fairly extensive scrutiny. Films are annotated with precise co-ordinates furnished by the AINS to assist this process, and may be fused with Elint to highlight areas of special interest. Unlike the front seat, which is 'still a vintage late 1950s, early 1960s layout with plenty of round dials and needles', the rear cockpit comprises a more modern, sophisticated layout 'which changes whenever a new sensor, nav system, or "def" system comes on board', to enable the RSO to manage the hi-tech sensors. Cameras carried in up to four bays in the chines and in the optional OBC 'glass' nose are believed to be in the 24-110in focal length range, supplied by Itek, Fairchild and Chicago Aerial Industries, such as the CAI Recon Optical 66in KS-127B and 110in CA-990 LOROPS; the former furnishes 1-2ft image resolution at stand-off distances of over 20nm, and the latter 5ft resolution at a staggering 150nm! Smaller 'mini-LOROPS' in the 24-36in range, such as Fairchild's F-924, may be used for more daring overflight manoeuvres. Colour, black and white or infra-red film may be carried. 'Solid' SR-71 noses come in two major configurations: ballast, used for training, and Loral synthetic aperture radar. The Loral payload allegedly used as near standard kit can produce photo-quality images of 3m resolution at oblique ranges of *at least* 30nm, unaffected by perspective which may render oblique camera or

infra-red shots unusable — a subject reconsidered in greater depth later in the book. Superheterodyne and interferometer Elint receivers packed in the forward fuselage cheeks near the core utility avionics U-Bay pick up and analyse enemy radar activity. All noses contain electromagnetic-sensitive threat warning receivers in noticeable bulges faired into the chines, retrofitted in the late 1970s as part of the SR-71's major digital self-defence upgrade package; as the SR-71 flies nose-up, these provide 360° coverage.

With sensor operation completed, at the far side of the loop the mission tape commands the SR' back towards home. Blackbirds eat up 150 miles of sky pulling a 30° bank, 180° turn at trisonic speed, but the pre-mission flightplan will have taken that into account. Still at Mach 3.2, cruising at 83,000ft, the beast will have expanded by up to 11in as temperatures reach 1,100°F in places. The 60lb of iron-ball black paint helps to dissipate 52°F of heat, though the glass in the canopies soak up a lot of friction. As one pilot put it: 'If you put your hand up to the canopy longer than three seconds you'll burn the heck out of it'. Squeeze-bottle baby-food-like rations are available for the crew to eat, but with a few minutes to spare while the instrument-scanning workload reduces to a more tolerable level, gazing at the beauty of the speckled dark blue celestial mural above or the blue-green curve of the Earth below provide a much more

inspiring pastime. Dan House: 'It is easy to see things on the ground like lakes, rivers, main highways, and on a clear day you can literally see hundreds of miles to the front and side. I made a turn over Des Moines, Iowa, one day at about 75,000ft. As I looked to the west I was looking down at Omaha, Nebraska, and could see Colorado. In instances like this it helps to have a working knowledge of geography and an active imagination'. Above, crews witness everything from shooting stars to the dazzling lights of the aurora borealis; and can get hooked!

Homeward Bound

After the system has put the Blackbird through the last waypoint and on direct path for the home 'drome, descent can begin in earnest. Again, this is done on autopilot at these speeds. Although highly skilled NASA pilots have handled Habus sans even SAS support, and held the bird within ±500ft of altitude, the possibility of overcontrol and pitch-up is all too serious a consideration; though pilots are well-versed with handling emergencies in the simulator. 'The improvement in safety over the first few years is the result of the learning curve and training. We have had a number of fairly serious emergencies and continue to have them, as is normal for any high-performance aircraft. What saves us is excellent planning and supervision, superlative aviators, and a vigorous preparation in the simulator. A typical comment after safe recovery of a serious emergency is "No big deal. I've done it/seen it/heard of it in the simulator."' One degree of pitch change equates with an altitude shift of 50ft/sec, and it's shockingly easy to get out of step with the desired inputs and get the Habu caught up in an unhealthy see-saw motion culminat-

Left:
March AFB, October 1980, and SR-71A 64-17975 rolls in, generating a huge, hazy trail from its hot airframe and engines. The drag parachute has been jettisoned but the doors will remain open until a new package is inserted later, back in the 'barn'. The bird will remain extremely hot for well over 20 minutes and Habu crews comment that they can actually hear the metal airframe contracting! *Frank B. Mormillo*

ing in the bird breaking up; crews privately develop their own quick way of pulling the tiger-striped bucket-mounted egress handle should all else fail!

To come down from bullet speed (in fact, slightly faster — a .30-06 rifle bullet manages a mere 3,000ft/sec), the throttles are retarded gradually through minimum afterburner to mil power, until they are half way back at Mach 2·5. Descent is typically 400ft/min in a 5° nose-down attitude. The inlet and bypass systems reverse their motions and the auto-fuel transfer pumps again shift the Habu's centre of gravity as speed and height drop off. At below FL 600 radio communication can be resumed and the RSO re-activates the IFF transponder to keep the friendly air defence forces happy.

Back down to FL 260, airspeed should be down to 400kt, and still winding down. The pilot is well and truly back in charge by this time, and another rendezvous for top-up may be on the tapes. This ballet between 'Q'-bird and thirsty Habu is often more challenging than the pre-Mach 3 refuelling. Crew fatigue is as big a consideration as the precision

required for a successful meet in three dimensions and, during night refuelling, pilots have reported powerful feelings of vertigo brought on by reflections of the tanker's lights in their goldfish bowl visors. SR-71 trainees undergo what are called hot departures to familiarise them with these problems, taking a fuel-laden Habu direct from the tarmac up to Mach 3+ at altitude then straight down to practice the hook-up in descent. Again, the Stratotanker makes most of the advances as the SR' driver lines up on the TACAN signal preparatory to the plug. Mid-sortie top-ups are also sometimes called for, and indefatigable crews have been known to fly missions of up to 10hrs duration. But as the tanks are purged of air as fuel burns off, using nitrogen fed from a pair of 105-litre capacity dewars to reduce flash-fire hazards and fuel sloshing, the aircraft could be said to be limited

Below:
Assisted by the PSD staff, a Habu crew exit their still-broiling steed for debrief and a well-earned rest. *Frank B. Mormillo*

solely by its nitrogen and oxygen stocks — though doubtless crews would add 'high-flyer's ****-ache' as another endurance limiter! Refuelling and purging processes have to be repeated once every two hours, the normal length of the 'hi' phase of the loop.

The descent and re-refuelling process are even more canned than in the ascent phase: partly as a means of standardising routines for safety via added familiarity and for more detailed critique of junior crew performance, but primarily as a noise abatement measure. When SAC began conducting its first trisonic SR-71 training flights over the US mainland in July 1967 the Command anticipated relatively few complaints compared to those received as a result of lower-altitude B-58 Hustlers and their quad array of noisy J79s. However, complaints there were, and in abundance: just under 3,000 in the first six months. The problem stemmed from supersonic descent to FL 260 and reacceleration to high Mach numbers during aerial refuelling manoeuvres. Congress subsequently mandated that the noisy Habus conduct their refuelling patterns over sparsely populated areas okayed by the FAA, or out at sea, off the West Coast. But the little-understood phenomena of secondary booms still causes problems: primary shockwaves from altitude are negligible, but when overlapped with secondary waves bouncing down off the upper atmosphere — as often occurs during even gentle turns, particularly over undulating topography where they can bunch up — the shockwaves can be revitalised to dramatic proportions. Huge booms can form, though often so local as to cover only a few hundred square metres. Cases of car windows popping out and greenhouses being wrecked have been blamed on visitors from mars and a host of other improbable causes, but are more likely the result of secondary sonic boom phenomena, or negligent primary ones. KC-10 Extender refuelling, a further 7,000ft up at around FL 330, has helped cure part of this problem, but Habu crews *must* attempt to minimise turns or drift during the supersonic ascent and descent phases. On the plus side, SR-71s have completed more than 20,000 in-flight refuellings with only one major accident, an excellent safety record.

On the correct vector for the home leg the pilot retards the throttles to just above idle to bleed off more height and get down to 275kt. After a long mission the crews will come straight in (and even ATC isn't going to stop them!); a shorter training hop will probably terminate in a pair of circuits to help cool the airframe and to squeeze in some practice approaches, over 10-15 minutes. On a post-operational hot arrival the bird comes straight in. The pilot raises the long nose to 10° pitch to reduce speed and the gear is popped out into the airstream to add drag and help cool off the tyres preparatory to the scrunch on terra firma. Lining up on the runway markers — most landings are composite, using ILS outputs on the ADI and making visual cross-checks through the windshield — the pilot plays with the throttles to bring his Blackbird within threshold speed limits. Touchdown is calculated at 155kt plus 1kt for every 1,000lb of fuel remaining over 10,000lb. Spilling JP7 through the dump on the tip of the snake's tail may be necessary if weight and speed are too hot. Final rudder and elevon inputs come into play as the stick-heavy SR-71 transitions back into the firm clutches of gravity. The sink rate is pretty dramatic and, viewed almost head-on, looks nothing short of a carrier approach as huge whisps of cloud vortex from the wing; these mark the low pressure suction of the upper surfaces which provide substantial lift on approach. Raising the nose in this way up to 12° on final to flare the machine cushions the blow, as does the enormous ground effect from the great steaming delta. As one pilot noted, 'It's *almost* impossible to perform a hard landing'. Dan House added: 'Flying the SR-71 at traffic pattern speeds and altitudes is a lot of work as the stick feel is heavy and the plane is not very responsive in pitch or roll. We also have angle of attack and "g" limits that prevent us from really pulling it around the sky. Our flare and landing technique is similar to most high-performance fighters. The difference is that we are going much faster, so we look like we are sinking and being saved by ground effect. The large delta wings push a cushion of air in front of the plane and we get into ground effect at about 25ft, so the plane is actually very easy to land acceptably. It is very difficult to land on speed at a specified point though — spot landings are tough.' With 11,000lb of fuel remaining the bird will squeal on the runway at 156kt, turning a wet ramp into an instant sauna as the machine rides on its main gear like an angry trident. As pitch drops off and the nosewheel nears the ground the pilot chops the power and flips the parachute deploy toggle, cueing a huge 40ft diameter 'chute which billows out from atop the tail empennage, drawn out by a pair of extraction 'chutes, 42in and 10ft wide, in sequence. SR-71 crews comment that 'unless you brace yourself or lock your harness your face may become part of the instrument panel'. One pilot described it as like 'walking into a wall at normal pace'. The orange blossom drags the Habu back to 100kt in a second, at which point a little brake input is required; and perhaps some extra runway too — the stopping distance for an SR' and its baby-smooth main gear tyres with a failed 'chute on a wet, slick runway is 2½ times that of a parabraked touchdown on a dry or grooved surface. When the ground speed reading cranks down to 60-55kt the pilot lets the 'chute go to avoid damage to the airframe from the necessarily tough lanyard which would follow after parasol deflation — not to mention getting the lines tangled in the rudders, another possible undesirable side-effect in strong cross-winds.

Some 5,000ft and a lot of noise, burnt rubber and expended kinetic later, the Habu is holding steady on idle. The pilot and RSO will put some slack into their harnesses but the $200,000 mission is not yet over; the RSO has to read out the thick wad of post-flight check-lists before the engines are spooled up and the Habu is permitted to trundle to the final stop-spot.

The considerable force of over a dozen ground technicians remains wary. While not glowing, the bird is still potentially lethal. As the beast cools so the airframe contracts and the noise is audible in the cockpit — a huge monster gorging itself on metal. 'You can actually hear the airplane groaning and creaking as the metal contracts' commented one pilot. Acute hearing! Another thought that was going too far and said that with the 'space helmet' on 'it is very unlikely that we could hear anything but massive compressor stalls, structural damage, or something else catastrophic'. However, it's possible to cut steak on the SR's leading wing edge and, if you like a really traditional high-flyer's breakfast, just pop a couple of eggs on the skin. Kelly's pride is a horror house to unwary Habu ground crew in the immediate post-sortie phase: inlet spikes are practically hypodermic and if the

OMS staff tapped the airframe in some ritualistic fashion they would end up stuck painfully to the hot skin. The machine is simply not approached. 10-15 minutes after a hot landing the power is still on idle to keep the crew and avionics air-conditioned. Groundcrew cautiously assist the cooling process by placing electric fans near the landing gear and uncranking bleed valves in the lower engine nacelles.

After 20 minutes at the stop spot the ground crew start to approach the cockpit with the boarding trolley. With the canopies flipped open and the steps hauled up against the port fuselage, the PSD crews assist their charges out of the bang seats. After a long high-Mach flight strapped in the seat the Habu drivers are apt to have jelly legs and the PSD will probably have to provide a shoulder for the exiting Habu crew to lean on. Once the pilot and his backseater are settled in the PSD van's necessarily luxurious armchairs, en route to the de-suiting area, the Habu is closed down; the displays lose any lingering trace of luminescence and the bird is towed nose-first back into the barn by tractor, for equipment down-loading, post-flight inspection and fluid reclamation before the machine's hydraulic nervous juices return to their near-solid state.

The inspection carried out by five structural specialists is thorough: every spot-weld on the airframe is meticulously examined in a process that consumes around six hours. The onboard Central Airborne Performance Analyzer (CAPA) assists this process by divulging the in-flight records of the performance of some 170 sub-systems for rapid isolation of faults. Back at the Wing building, the aircrew will have completed debrief, having provided mission details (helped by the down-loaded mission tapes) and the status of the aircraft (any systems glitches to underline the CAPA read-out, to help the Habu tweakers), and will be going home for a well-earned rest. The marriage between front and back seater is a solid relationship — it has to be if the team are to do the job at hand — and many aircrews joke that they spend more time with each other than with their families! Given their enthusiasm and dedication, it must be a *very* rewarding job.

Above:
Dwarfed by the gargantuan tow tractor, SR-71A 64-17975 is pulled back to its 'barn' for hydraulic fluid reclamation, sensor and mission tape down-loading and a thorough post-flight visual inspection. *Frank B. Mormillo*

Below:
Dressed in their David Clark Co S1030 'gold suits', a Habu crew stroll from their aircraft following a mission. Traditionally a male preserve, Blackbird cockpit vacancies might soon become open to 'petticoat pilots' if Congresswoman Beverly Byron's new Bill is successful. *USAF*

Lockheed SR-71

SR-71A

SR-71B and SR-71C

SR-71A

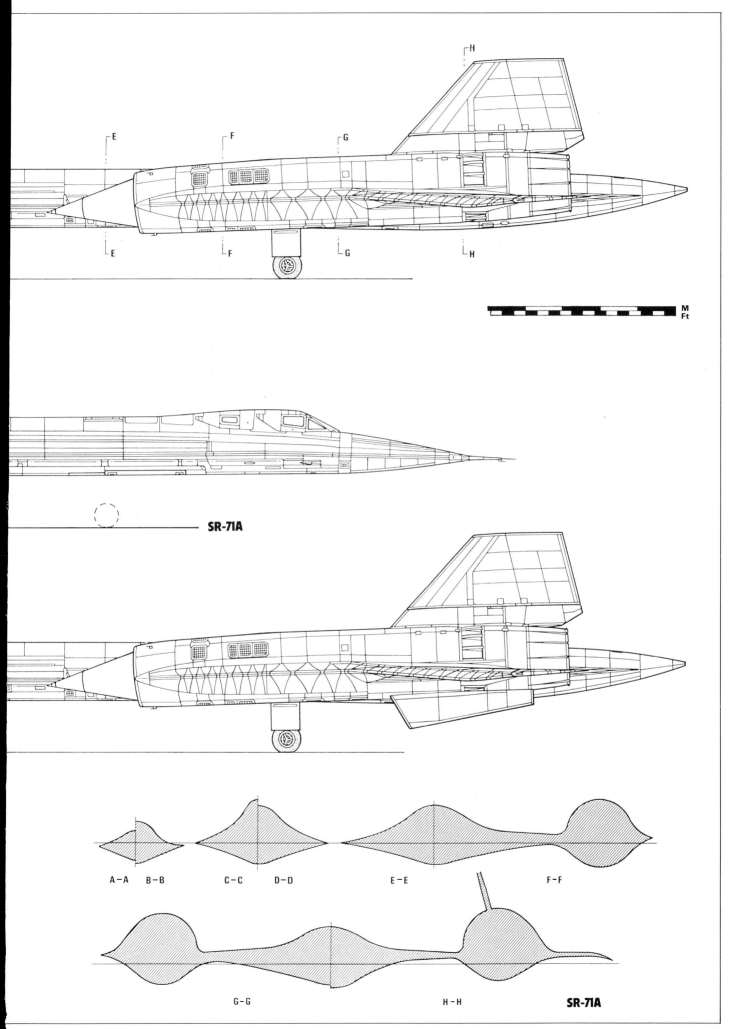

E F G H

SR-71A

A–A B–B   C–C D–D   E–E   F–F

G–G   H–H   **SR-71A**

Lockheed SR-71A

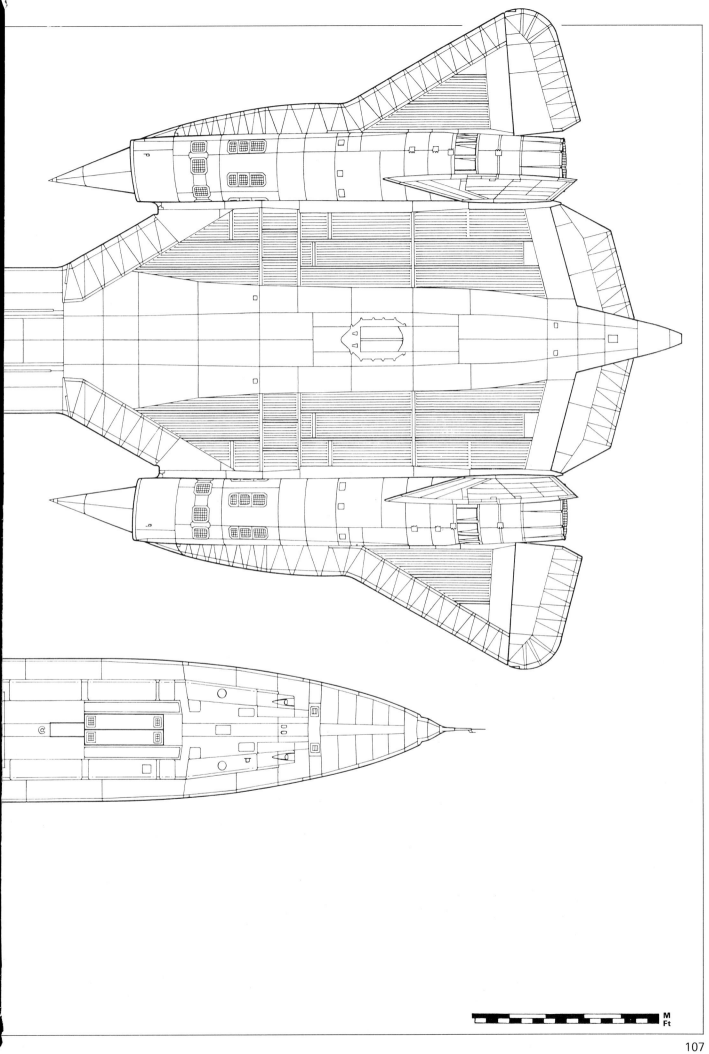

6
'Kickers'

Situated some four miles northwest of Huntingdon in the heart of the Cambridgeshire countryside, RAF Alconbury plays host to some of USAFE's most unique aircraft. Eighteen Northrop F-5Es from the 527th Tactical Fighter Training 'Aggressor' Squadron make like MiGs, performing DACT in a carnival parade of colour schemes, while at the other side of the base the much more sinister-looking black outlines of the 95th Reconnaissance Squadron, 17th RW's Lockheed TR-1As loom in and out of view. Presently commanded by Col Arthur Saboski, the 17th is a SAC tenant unit falling within USAFE jurisdiction complete with full independent maintenance, PSD, staff and intelligence resources. Maintenance teams comprise SAC's traditional three components: the 17th AMS, responsible for mission equipment and Dragon Lady black boxes, the 17th FMS, which performs ongoing work on aircraft flight control systems and structure, and the 17th OMS, which handles flight-line servicing, embracing launch and recovery assistance under the aegis of skilled crew chiefs. Working hand-in-hand with the 17th RW's own intelligence and debrief outfit are an even more secret data-processing division, from USAF's Electronic Security Command (ESC) — the 6952nd ESS, subordinate to Electronic Security, Europe (headquartered at Ramstein, AB, West Germany, alongside the 17th RW's parent Air Division, the 7th AD).

SAC is very statistically orientated and Lt-Col Mick Uramkin's TR-1A

Below:
The alluring shape of TR-1A 80-1086 in its hangar at RAF Alconbury in July 1987. *Authors*

jockeys refer to their unit as 'the 95th', though their flight suits are emblazoned with the distinctive kicking donkey patch. Quizzed on what nickname they use, one pilot offered a suitable unofficial title: 'The Ass Kickers'! The insignia certainly reflects the stubborn handling characteristics of Lockheed's Dragon Lady, the resolute qualities of the flyers, and the dramatic, positive effect their mission would have upon NATO integrity if the 'Kickers' had to buck for real.

The 17th was established at Alconbury on 1 October 1982, working up with people and facilities prior to the fly-over of Stateside-based TR-1As, at the time forming an initial cadre of three aircraft and nine pilots within the 9th SRW; elements of the British popular press preferred to believe that the unit would be based at Greenham Common with all the other sinister and controversial objects

which were occupying their attention at the time. The 17th leaned on nearby Mildenhall's Det 4, which was in the process of winding down its U-2R activities and solitary TDY Black Angel, transferring the aircraft and certain items of support equipment along with vital know-how in the form of the skilled Lockheed tech-reps. The first TR-1A, 80-1068, arrived to a welcoming reception on 12 February 1983, followed by pair-mate 80-1070 trailing close behind. Both flew the gruelling 5,600-mile, 12½hr trans-American & Oceanic hop non-stop from Beale, and went on to fly their first missions the following Wednesday, four days later; while 1 March marked an important milestone when CO of the opening era, Col Thomas C. Lesan, proudly announced that the 17th RW had been declared operational.

By October 1985 six aircraft were on strength and five of the new hangars well advanced in construction on the north side of the base. Considerable runway work was required, particularly in widening taxiways for the wide-span, wide-turning TR-1A. The airfield was closed for part of 1982 for this work. The force has continued to grow cumulatively, adding an average of two TR-1As and a larger number of crews annually, though several aircraft have come and gone on special TDY evaluation assignments from California lasting an average of three months apiece, while selected airframes have been exchanged for newer production aircraft, as older examples return to Palmdale for

depot-level maintenance and avionics updates or repairs; people and planes change, with pilots rotating in for a three-year tour. The unit is still very much in flux, with nine aircraft on strength (mid-1987), and will not reach its full authorised unit establishment of 14 aircraft until 1989, by which time the expanded facilities should be ready, as part of £15 million-worth of building modifications and improvements to the base — including the more convenient relocation of the 95th HQ and Squadron centre from the west to the east side of the main runway, adjacent to the voluminous TR-1A hangars.

Despite the obvious attraction to the staff, tech-reps, PSD and intelligence community of being co-located with nearby Mildenhall and its similar, if not identical, command and back-up organisation, many high-flyers wonder why such a site was chosen. The prevailing wind frequently runs across the runway at above cross-wind limits and on 13 January 1987, for example, temperatures in Huntingdon got as low as −14°C, making the strip very slippery — though doubtless take-offs into the thick cool air were more dramatic than usual! To ease the cross-wind problem it was hoped that the cross-runway 05/23 could be returned to use but this would entail much expensive work and would not be available before 1990. These conditions form a stark contrast to sunny Beale and a major change of routine for newcomers to Alconbury, whose talents had been honed in

warm air stuffed with thermals. Chasing a TR-1A in one of the new five-litre Fords as 'mobile' can also be a new experience on a wet ramp, not to mention the skill required in placing a zero-track, eight-ton Black Lady on a slick runway in cross-winds. 'Kickers' pilot Steve Randle, who has been in the programme for five years, just under three of those at Alconbury, noted, 'diversions for weather, particularly due to cross-winds, are something that we get a lot more practice at around here than we'd like to. We don't use Wethersfield — the runway is in very poor condition down there. We can use Bedford but we prefer to go to Lakenheath and Mildenhall, both for proximity and because they have certain ground equipment that is compatible with us over there. We also use Wyton [a RAF Canberra PR9 recce outfit] which is very close. Sometimes we're fortunate to get whatever we can get!' The unit operated out of Wyton in the spring of 1984 when Alconbury's runways were under repair. Bedford has occasionally hosted aircraft on overnight stops and Wethersfield was visited up to January 1984.

Watching TR-1As in circuit around the base, observers can be forgiven for the mistaken impression that the 'Kickers' close all their missions with a spiral descent. Air traffic in eastern England is heavy, and there are occasions which may prove it necessary to perform such a let-down, but the pilots consider it a 'waste of time'. Rather, such circuitous manoeuvres are part of lo-altitude proficiency sorties, geared to provide a series of practice approaches from holding altitude and max climb bolters, so that the pilots keep on the ball with the Dragon Lady's hairy landing characteristics. Staff do not distinguish between the various sorties: pilots are credited with a mission regardless of its nature — operational ho-alt, or hi- or lo-alt proficiency. Steve Randle: 'All missions, whether it's an operational mission or by design a training sortie, are counted as a training credit. We have a requirement to get x number of hi missions, x number of lo missions

Left:
Abradable wingtip skids and the threat warning receiver pod protrude from TR-1A 80-1067's port wingtip. This aircraft has served at both Beale and Alconbury, and is pictured here at Edwards AFB in October 1982.
Frank B. Mormillo

per month, but we don't differentiate. I'd be hard pressed to come up with a ratio; just by the whim of the scheduler or chance, you may get a couple of long operational sorties a month, in which case the vast majority of the flying time is going to be operational time as opposed to training-only — but you could go to the next month and not get an operational sortie at all and all your flying time would be training.' Lo-alt training does have the advantage that pilots need not be bedecked in full pressure paraphernalia, and all the pre-flight suiting-up that that entails. Standard fighter pilot kit of light-weight grey plastic hat and green flightsuit is the norm, avoiding S1010B-related fatigue during the heavy stick control phases of repeated practice approaches; more on which later. Aircraft not assigned to an operational mission wear standard slick noses and Superpods or clean wings, so that fewer than four of the 'Kickers' TR-1As are fully mission-capable at any one time. But as things hot up, that would change: 'As world tensions change, like any aircraft you would bring up your airplanes to their wartime capabilities; we would obviously prepare ourselves for whatever situation and get as many aircraft operationally mission-capable as possible.'

Stan-Eval (Standardisation and Evaluation) sorties are scheduled annually, when one of the 'Tamers' TR-1Bs flies over for a series of two-seat checkrides, but despite only single-seaters being on hand for routine training for most of the year, very high standards are maintained. Staff keep a watchful eye on the crews, and the pilots themselves have their own scoring system for such facets of the sorties as the landing phase. Steve Randle: 'We have in fact recently had a relatively new pilot here at Alconbury who didn't fly for a while because of sickness. Over a period of sorties it was observed that he had difficulties — sort of lost the picture and wasn't up to stuff as far as landing was concerned — and we ended up sending him back to Beale for some more training. Unfortunately we lack a two-seat airplane here which makes it fairly hard to evaluate and standardise in-flight performance.' Landing mishaps at Alconbury with the tricky long-spanned jets are a relatively rare occurrence given the far from ideal weather conditions, though at least one aircraft was damaged during the early work-up phase: 80-1069 suffered an accident on 18 October 1983 when it was struck by a vehicle, damaging one

wing quite severely. Like other TR-1As and U-2Rs that have had some rough treatment, the machine was dismantled and airlifted back to Palmdale in a C-5 Galaxy for repairs (returning to its operational unit 3½ months later with a small red bus 'kill' marking on its right undercarriage door to commemorate the scrape). Aircraft 80-1066 came over to cover for the absence, though '69 had to return to Palmdale for a further year's sick leave in 1985-86.

Total hours clocked up by the 95th varies considerably according to weather and survey demands from higher authority — pilots *can* get as little as four-to-five hours per month. Around 18-20 hours is average for a line pilot, slightly less for a staff pilot, but as each sortie draws upon a buddy pilot as back-up, this means crews must be prepared to fly two sorties a week. Monthly high-timers clock up as much as 33 hours.

Mission profile
Operational missions task the aircraft to the edge of the Iron Curtain, to monitor the Warsaw Pact's military posture. Major border exercises can be monitored to help survey enemy tactics — of vital importance to the Army — and signals information picked up to help analyse the Eastern Bloc's Electronic Order of Battle (EOB). Such an operational sortie begins on the day prior to flight. Two pilots prepare for each mission, a routine which has endured throughout the U-2's career. One will make the flight, the other is the standby pilot. This arrangement is necessary for two reasons; one is medical, the other that flying the TR-1A is actually a two-man job in the pre-take-off and landing phases. Long, high-altitude flights require a fit pilot and he gets a thorough medical from the PSD immediately before each flight. Temperature, blood

pressure, diet, pulse and weight are recorded and checked before the Dragon rider is passed fit to fly. Descending from altitude with blocked Eustachian tubes, for example, can cause anything from a severe headache to black-out. A second pilot is prepared to step in should any of the medical parameters miss the mark, but the back-up prefers to have as much warning as possible if the main man is feeling off colour. Psychological preparation for the flight is important too and it's nice to know the day before if you are likely to face a session in the cockpit in lieu of a pilot with the sniffles. Initial planning of a flight obviously depends on the sensor load, mission

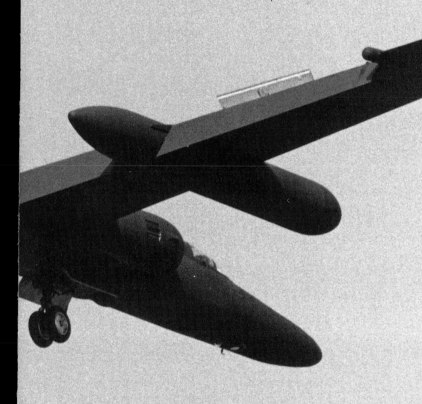

Above:
Superpod-equipped TR-1A 80-1085 in the circuit over Mildenhall in 1987. The high-drag configuration is used to bring the aircraft to the required 'T-speed' for touch-down. *John Dunnell*

Right:
The Dragon Lady's solid tail wheel unit is linked direct to the rudder pedals via cables and pulleys, a weight-saving measure in keeping with Kelly Johnson's KISS philosophy — 'Keep it Simple, Stupid'. This unit takes the initial strain on landing. Interiors of gear doors, intakes and hatches are coloured zinc chromate. *Authors*

Below:
TR-1A 80-1069 taxying to the take-off point with stabilising pogo legs installed. These units can swivel through 360° in their sockets and free-fall from the wings on take-off. *T. Shia (Enterprise Aviation Publications)*

Right:
A close-up of the all-important pogo outrigger on TR-1A 80-1086. Also just visible is the aft-facing ECM pod faired into the trailing edge of the starboard wing. *Authors*

duration and the area in which surveillance is to be supplied. Whatever the prospective scenario, precise route planning and careful designing of race-track orbits behind the Forward Edge of the Battle Area (FEBA) are prerequisites. More detailed briefing follows on mission day, around two hours before lift-off. The 95th's briefing area seems surprisingly large for a one-man, one-aircraft mission. In fact the session includes intelligence officers, probably people from the 17th AMS or OMS, and the back-up pilot, of course. A TR-1A mission generates quite a lot of work, but it produces a lot of data too.

When the details are agreed the pilot then moves to the suiting-up area, care of the PSD. Though more comfortable than the restricting MC-2 and MC-3 partial pressure suits worn by earlier U-2 crews, the David Clark Co S1010B is still a formidable garment. In fact, suit is a modest word to describe over $10,000 worth of hi-tech life preservation, and each pilot has two suits for his personal use. The layers of material, starting with cotton next to the skin, nylon pressurisation mesh and insulated rubberised layers, add up to 3in to the pilot's girth. The garment has built-in boots, flame-resistant, gold-coloured outer cover and integral sealed helmet and gloves, all pressurised. Over it go the parachute harness, self-inflating life preservers and outer flying boots. Once the helmet is fitted to its circular capstan neck seal the mission has effectively commenced, for it remains in place, with the clear visor sealed, for anything up to 13hrs from that point. In flight a series of tinted vizors can also be lowered to reduce glare. Apart from the modest 'dymo' name tape stuck on the helmet, any semblance of individuality or squadron decoration is tempo-

rarily submerged, though personalised 'Flag' patches can be attached to velcro shoulder pads.

Surprisingly, most crewmen have few objections to this world of space-suited privation. Maj Bob Uebelacker, who has flown the Dragon Lady for 4½ years, most of that time at Blackbirdsville, Beale, rates it as comfortable in the cabin. He discounts tales of aspiring U-2/TR-1 jocks running in horror from the programme after wearing the rubber monster. In the last 10 years of training at Beale only one individual was washed-out due to suit claustrophobia. That happened during the

Above:
TR-1A 80-1078 about to go airborne at Greenham Common in 1985. The wings have flexed up and the pogos have clattered to the tarmac (one of which can be seen tumbling away near the jetpipe). *John Dunnell*

Below:
The Dragon Lady climbs out at an impressive 25-30° pitch, rising on the 17,000lb st developed by the Pratt & Whitney J75/P-13B. *John Dunnell*

temporary suspension of a section of the interview process when candidates are expected to sit in the suit for a free one-hour trial period. However, even Bob Uebelacker admitted that the suit is a real handicap on the ground when attempting to walk or climb steps. Once in the cockpit, with air-conditioning in operation and minimal physical demands, the extra weight of the helmet is the only reminder of the constraints.

Before embarking on his slow moon-walk from PSD van to cockpit, the pilot has to spend at least an hour in the suit pre-breathing. Stretched out in a special reclining brown

High-flyer Maj Bob Uebelacker and TR-1A 80-1086. Only the crew chiefs are assigned particular aircraft: pilots come to grips with a selection of machines as they fly the various sensor and training configurations on operational and proficiency sorties. *Authors*

armchair, he takes the weight off his feet and breathes pure oxygen. This lengthy pre-breathing period is necessary to achieve zero nitrogen pressure in all parts of the body, especially areas with low blood flow or high fat content where nitrogen is more easily retained. Like divers, TR-1 pilots can suffer from decompression (the bends) if even small traces of dissolved nitrogen are allowed to form bubbles in the body. The symptoms of this phenomenon are variously unpleasant, ranging from patches of hot, itching (but inaccessible) skin to severe pains in the joints. In the worst cases, restricted breathing, cyanosis, partial paralysis or even coma may be experienced. An individual pilot's pre-breathing time may vary a little, but on completion he heads for the PSD van to be driven to his black bird in another reclining chair. Oxygen flow is maintained through a yellow portable unit and the rapid build-up of body heat inside the suit is controlled by an air-conditioning function in the same box. A PSD operative carries the unit to the cockpit with the pilot connected via the two supply umbilicals entering his suit. When he is settled in the TR-1A's office and connected to the aircraft's own oxygen and air-conditioning systems it is important to have the engine running. Until this is done using an external ground starter — the 'huffer' — there is no cooling air to the suit apart from what the yellow pack can supply. Temperatures can build up rapidly, exhausting the pilot, so a 'howdah' sunshade is attached to the aircraft entry step unit to keep the area cool. This may not be necessary at Alconbury, but temperatures can often exceed 100°F at Beale. Pilots often lose 6-7lb per flight as it is!

Right:

Site 5, Plant 42, Palmdale. Fitters install the all-moving tail into the TR-1's rear empennage. This whole assembly can move through an arc of 5° for pitch trim, a feature used only by the ER-2, TR-1 and U-2R models. *Lockheed*

Above:
**A J75-P-13B engine in the Pratt &
Whitney production shop. The oil tank,
which wraps around the forward low
pressure turbine section, has yet to be
fitted.** *Pratt & Whitney*

In order to reduce the pre-flight time and the pilot's workload on the ground, he steps into a virtually flight-ready aircraft. The cockpit checks, walk-around inspection, punching of waypoints into the INS and paperwork are all done by the reserve pilot, or 'mobile'. After groundcrew have strapped the pilot in, he performs about half a dozen checks, such as ensuring that the fold-away rudder pedals are correctly adjusted and the LOX system is satisfactory, and he's ready to go. The 'mobile' stays on the access platform while the pilot's leg-restraint 'spurs' are attached to the Lockheed zero-zero ejection seat. This lightweight unit bears a family resemblance to the F-104's C-2 seat, but is far more capable. Early ejection problems have been overcome by canopy penetrators on the seat and large bullet-like canopy ejectors, visible near the base of the canopy bow. The first U-2As had no ejection facility at all. With everything ticking over, the Starfighter-style sideways-hinged canopy is swung shut and the 'mobile' officer retreats to his powerful chase car. From then on the significance of his 'mobile' designation is clearer. From the vantage point of his blue Ford he supervises the Dragon Lady's stately progress to the runway via a UHF radio link. Her unusual undercarriage and immense, drooping wings mean that everything has to be right at this stage. A wrong turn could mean an aborted mission. Ex-bomber pilots like Bob Uebelacker may be at a slight advantage in this game.

Turn radius on the ground is usually a little under 300ft, increased if cross-winds are acting against the turn by pushing the tall vertical tail the wrong way. Slightly slack rigging of the manually-operated cables which control the steerable, solid tail wheels can also exacerbate this problem. While this ponderous process takes place the second chase vehicle does a FOD inspection of the runway.

On the runway centreline with final cockpit checks done, the Lady is ready to roll. In case anyone imagines that this is a quiet, docile sailplane of some kind, the full-blooded bellow of the J75 at this point is a reminder of the latest 17,000lb st punch of that well-established powerplant. Steve Randle was well used to its habits in his previous tour on the F-106 and he regards it as a reliable unit. (Most of the engines are in fact recycled by P&W from previous service in F-105 Thunderchief and F-106 Delta Dart fighters.) Spool-up time is a little slower than that of more recent designs and there is no afterburner to cover for the few seconds of delay in response. There is certainly no lack of kick on take-off, though. Even a fully-laden aircraft has to be carefully trimmed to avoid over-rotation. Take-off run varies from a maximum 1,500ft to a third of that for a lightly-loaded lady on a proficiency circuit. Climb-out is always impressive, even at around 112kt; the aircraft appears to rise vertically on its smoke trail from certain angles. Bob Uebelacker explained: 'Initial take-off is pretty spectacular because thrust at sea-level is a lot higher than it is at altitude. In fact the older airplanes were even more impressive. The old C-model could stand on its tail!'

On a pilot's first few training hops at Beale the outboard pogo wheels may be left in place, but normally their safety pins will be removed on the 'last chance' check. They are able to swivel 360° in their sockets on the deck, but their weight causes them to free-fall from the wings once the aircraft starts to lift. The red and white units are then retrieved by the attendant Dodge pick-up for re-use.

A steep climb-out is maintained to keep the aircraft within stress limits and from then on it is difficult to prevent it from heading for the heights. TR-1 is flown at what is termed a 'constant cruise climb' as fuel burns off and weight reduces. As operational altitude is reached the climb angle falls from an initial 25-30° to 5-10° pitch in the thinner, upper air.

Power is kept at 90-95% after take-off and the aircraft enters a 'Mach schedule' above 50,000ft to keep the airspeed within limits. Normally this would involve a Mach 0·72 cruise at altitude, with a much wider stall margin than the 6-7kt 'coffin corner' or earlier U-2s. Steve Randle indicated that it is something over 10kt now. The upper limit for all models is Mach 0·8. Definition of operational

Below:
TR-1A 80-1067 in flight over the western United States during a Lockheed test flight, with clean wings. TR-1As used for low-altitude proficiency training are configured in this manner with the ballast-type, basic nose. *Lockheed*

altitude is always contentious but an average figure of about 75,000ft in battle configuration is reliable: the big wing of the U-2R/TR-1 can give it equivalent altitude performance to the early U-2As, taking it up to 78,000ft. There are isolated reports of lightly-loaded aircraft exceeding 81,000ft.

Autopilot is used for the greater part of the cruise and this manages most control functions, including trim. On the U-2R/TR-1 airframe the vertical and horizontal stabilisers move as one unit for trim purposes, pivoting around the forward spar of the latter within the tail empennage. This provides an arc of 5° for trim, indicated by the white 'V' at the base of the fin's leading edge and pitch markers forward of the horizontal tail.

There is a pitch trim switch on the right of the control yoke which sets the position of the stabilisers via a hydraulic actuator. Manual trim is possible at all altitudes and airspeeds; the idea is to reduce loads on the tail — always the most vulnerable part of the U-2 family's anatomy. The pilot-operated gust-flap system also takes the strain off the tail section, mainly in the descent phase of flight when turbulence may be encountered. The U-2R/TR-1 are also fitted with double spoilers above the wings. An inboard pair can be raised 60° at airspeeds below 110kt in the descent phase, while the outer set assist in roll control at low altitude where large bank-angles cannot be used. Bank angles of 20° on autopilot and 45° on command represent reasonable figures for standard use, but are not limits. Most of the later U-2Rs had a set of external ribs fitted above the horizontal stabiliser as stiffeners. Their purpose is to reduce fatigue problems caused by airflow buffeting associated with the Superpods. TR-1 has the same beef-up but it is internal. Another visual difference between the U-2R and TR-1 is the small portion of fixed wing trailing edge between the TR-1's to accommodate the Superpods. The U-2R requires modification to its continuous flap area if the pods are fitted.

Those who have examined the TR-1/U-2 cockpit often express surprise at the bomber-sized proportions of the control yoke, seemingly anomalous in a fighter-type cockpit. Emphasis on weight-saving has always ruled out powered controls and the big-winged aircraft's hand-

Top left:
This is about as close to the Dragon Lady's office as most people are allowed to venture; all the same, the cockpit fan is clearly in view, as are the rear-view mirrors, drift sight and (just under the console coaming on the right-hand side) the digital threat warning display. *Frank B. Mormillo*

Centre left:
A tail shot of U-2R 68-10340, with air-brakes, tail wheel unit and radar warning receiver (on the tail cone) in view. The U-2R and TR-1 models utilise different threat warning installations. *Frank B. Mormillo*

Left:
Airbrake detail on the U-2R. The airbrake and interior is matt black, with a white actuating cylinder and steel-coloured tubing. Wires are steel coloured. *Frank B. Mormillo*

117

ling characteristics demand large aileron control inputs; hence the big stick. At operational speed and altitude, control response is more sensitive, but energetic. Full-travel movements are often necessary lower down, especially in cross-wind conditions; the Cessna T-37 is a good trainer to prepare pilots for this type of handling. Physical strains of this kind are an unwelcome addition to the already heavy workload involved in flights which can last for over 12 hours and (theoretically) up to 6,000+ miles. The S1010B suit is not normally pressurised in flight, though it would inflate instantly if its automatic sensor detected a loss of cabin pressure. It has been calculated that a pilot would be conscious for about three seconds in the event of sudden decompression, allowing no time to secure a visor or suit opening. In slightly longer than this he would suffer the hideous symptoms of above Armstrong's line (63,000ft). Here, all body fluids (including blood) would literally boil. The suit is therefore secured at all times, with consequent restrictions on movement. Aircrew devise their own ingenious methods of overcoming these handicaps. Steve Randle, who at the time of the authors' visit had just flown with Bob Uebelacker as his 'mobile', described one such feat of inventiveness: 'Bob put a spare pencil someplace. I didn't need it and I put it back into the case which we stow on the right side of the cabin next to the seat. My particular technique for doing this is to take the dividers which we carry in a place on the yoke.

I take the pointy end of the dividers and stick it in the eraser of the pencil, using that as an extension to get it back in the case, because I can't reach it with the bulky glove.' Even these elaborate moves would be ruled out with an inflated suit. Pilots have occasional emergency procedure practices in pressure chambers under these conditions.

Having reached his orbit zone the pilot then settles into a lengthy surveillance span. When Geoffrey Pattie, then Under Secretary of State for the RAF, announced the establishment of the American 95th RS at Alconbury, his brief read: 'The aircraft will provide timely tactical reconnaissance information in all weathers about the deployment and movement of enemy forces in a time of crisis or war. This will reduce the likelihood of surprise attack and enable NATO commanders to deploy their own forces in the best way to resist aggression.' In practice, this is pretty much what the 'Kickers' do. Their various sensor configurations (discussed later) can be employed anywhere, above any sort of cloud-base. The aircraft's race-track orbit would normally be positioned behind

the FEBA, with the autopilot and INS in charge. (The faith TR-1A pilots have in their Litton inertial navigator is exemplified by the pride of place given to a framed photo of the black box control panel in the 95th RS briefing room!) Under exceptional circumstances, possibly to assess strike damage, the pilot might be required to venture beyond the relative safety of friendly airspace, but it is unlikely that such a valuable target would be risked in this way. In so doing it could be put within SAM range, particularly the SA-12 which is reputedly capable of hacking down anything within a 60-mile radius. Fighters obviously can't be discounted either, even behind the FEBA. Steve Randle: 'So long as I can stay on this side of the FEBA, which I'm going to do unless they have some high priority something that I don't know about — in which case I'm not going to volunteer!; no, I'll do what I've got to do — the SAMs should not be a threat. The fighters are the biggest threat to me because they can come over and get me and maybe make it back across the border before they get got.' Asked whether the aircraft is self-sufficient in ECM, Bob Uebelacker commented 'We take anything we can get'. This could involve the whole gamut of electronic protection, including EF-111A, and the direct protection of Eagles eager for MiG bait under the control of the other orbiting 'prize' the E-3 AWACS Sentry. The Dragon Lady, however, is anything but a sitting duck. It can pull relatively hard 2·5g manoeuvres at altitude, out-turning any fighter and

Above:
U-2R 68-10336 over Palmdale with the ASARS-2 test installation. Note the beefed-up, ribbed, horizontal tail peculiar to the 'R' model; the TR-1's tail incorporates internal stiffeners. The 'washing-up bowl' antenna just aft of the Q-Bay is believed to be a satellite communications link. *Lockheed*

creating homing problems for the most tenacious missile in the thin upper air.

Automatic operation of the TR-1A's sensor packages, developed out of experience of 'Senior Book', means that the pilot may well have comparatively little to do while his Dark Lady goes about her business. Mainly, it is a matter of switching equipment on and making adjustments. 'We've finally got most of our buttons, switches and dials glove-sized rather than pinkie-finger size so we can manipulate them', observed Steve. There are also procedures for coping with malfunctions and there is the possibility of getting a pilot to reposition switches. On the other hand, it is quite possible to fly the entire mission, door-to-door, in complete radio silence if necessary. The minimal workload is dictated partly by physical factors too. Bob finds that 'you can get real tired if you have to exert yourself. It's amazing how tired you can get if you have to hand-fly it a great deal'. High altitude glare is another problem which would not occur to most people. The intensity of the sun poses real problems at 70,000ft+. With the TR-1A in one posture for long periods the sun can over-heat part of the suit, or cause tiring glare through the 'fish-bowl' helmet, even with tinted visors. There is a painted-on sunshade over a large part of the canopy and an adjustable shade which attaches to the canopy bow inside. Even these can be insufficient and Steve Randle's famous ingenuity finds solutions here too. He uses three map-boards sup-

ported by the right cockpit mirror, the cockpit fan, the canopy bow and glareshield. 'I build a sort of house of cards there. Let's face it, there's not much other traffic at altitude so I don't have to look out and see what's coming! I manage to build a tent of shade in there.' Given that a 5th, 95th or 99th Dragon Lady driver might well spend anything up to 100 hours a year at altitudes in excess of 70,000ft, solar radiation is theoretically a major hazard; one which the crews take seriously, but one which Bob Uebelacker feels is kept well in check. 'In fact there was a study not too long ago when I was back at Beale. There was some concern about radiation hazards, especially during sunspot activity, and they actually did some tests where they put some dose meters in the suits and the guys went up; but there was not much difference from the background radiation you get down here. With the canopy and the suit on and the helmet with a tinted visor we didn't experience a radiation problem.' Scheduling pilots for extensive lo-alt proficiency sorties mitigates the problem further, and the oblique insolation in the NATO operating latitudes also helps provide

some degree of added protection — nature's own sun lotion.

Duration of flights varies and nine hours is the limit beyond which discussion becomes sensitive. It is known that earlier U-2s could manage over 10 hours, and the U-2R/TR-1 have the same engine, with increased weight but greater wing area and over 1,200gal of extra fuel. It is possible to estimate mission duration of over 13 hours covering more than 6,000 miles. Contrary to popular mythology, this would all be done with the power on. U-2 pilots have never voluntarily glided anywhere except in an emergency. Steve Randle's succinct comment on that possibility was: 'If the engine's off, the pilot's heart is palpitating!' In practice, it is the human factors which set realistic limits again. The longest trip most 95th RS men might be expected to fly is the direct ferry run from Beale to Alconbury, either delivering or returning a plane. This is a 5,600-mile trip and it can be done in less than 13 hours at a ground-speed of around 430kt.

Remaining virtually immobile in a cockpit for that length of time is undoubtedly a salutary experience. The pilot can, if he wishes, pass the time by experimenting with the famous food warmer. Processed foods are supplied in containers resembling toothpaste tubes with long plastic nozzles. These are inserted through a pressurised valve in the 'chin-strap' area of the helmet and squeezed in the appropriate direction. Pre-heating can be done in a unit on the left instrument console. However,

visions of bored pilots gorging themselves on a vast menu of popsicle-sized banquets are wide of the mark. Bob Uebelacker's verdict: 'I personally don't use it. I haven't found anything that's worth eating, that's warm. I stick to the apple sauces, peaches and pears. Beef and gravy just gets to my stomach.' Steve is not a regular at the Dragon Lady diner either. 'I find it equally unappetising. I've been in the programme five years now and I have never used the food heater. But just a few months ago I decided I ought to experience it just once, so I took along a new soup: clam chowder. A new listing on the menu! I have to count it a great success because the tube didn't explode as they sometimes will. So I used it exactly once. I'll never use it again.' It is also worth mentioning here that there are no onboard arrangements for disposal of anything other than liquid human waste, down a pee tube. Pilots take a low residue diet in the period prior to a mission, just like their Mach 3 Habu colleagues.

As the flight enters its final stages the pilot's skills are very necessary once again. Despite the fatigue of a lengthy trip he has to tackle the hardest part of any U-2/TR-1 sortie: getting the thing down safely. The descent, like the ascent, is a carefully planned process which takes around half an hour. Navigation into the last leg has to be as precise as ever. Nav controls are grouped on the right console. The downward-looking Baird driftsight may be of some use in checking position at any stage, although its large cross-haired display in the upper part of the instrument panel is more likely to reveal only cloud patterns in the European scenario. Earlier aircraft had an upward-directed periscope/sextant for taking starshots but this was

removed as inertial systems improved. The remaining optical components project an image of the terrain beneath the aircraft using a series of mirrors and prisms in the periscope tube. A scanning head, projecting slightly from the lower forward fuselage, can be rotated through 360° using a handle in the cockpit. It is used extensively in areas where cloud cover is thinner.

Careful engine management is needed in the descent to avoid flame-out, using a planned Engine Pressure Ratio schedule and open engine bleed valves. This cuts Exhaust Pressure Ratio (EPR) from about 2·30 at altitude to 2·08 and eventually to an idle pressure yielding an airspeed of 150-170kt (depending on air conditions). Faster descent speeds can be used in smooth air. Flaps, airbrakes and undercarriage are lowered early to generate drag, with the gust control setting operative to reduce elevator load forces on the yoke. The pilot also has to remember the canopy de-icing routine as he enters denser, moister air. The cockpit fan can be switched on to help circulate warm air and avoid a frosted canopy — the transparencies have to be pre-heated to

avoid humid air freezing on them. Bob stressed the importance of this job: 'If there is any kind of humidity you could get a glaze on the windshield which can get your attention when you're coming in to land. I learned that fairly early in my training phase when I forgot to do that and it's very difficult to see outside.' Icing problems don't adversely affect the rest of the airframe. Moisture in the air tends to freeze on the cold, fuel-bearing sections of the wing producing a very thin glaze resembling white condensation.

All being well, the TR-1A should reach a point about 10 miles out and around 2,000ft in altitude for the glidepath to landing. Its pilot is still fully occupied for he now has to perform two more crucial operations: calculating landing speed and balancing fuel in the wings. A 'T-speed' formula is used to establish the correct landing speed for the prevailing conditions. 'T' stands for the threshold speed which the TR-1A should have crossing the runway threshold. It is based on the zero-fuel weight of the aircraft plus a knot for every remaining hundred gallons of fuel. (The TR-1 does at least have a reasonably detailed digital fuel-

remaining display; the gauge in early U-2s resembled that of an old family saloon.) In gusty conditions around Alconbury another 3kt might well be added for safety as the 9,000ft runway provides plenty of stopping-room. Stall speed is around 10kt below 'T-speed'. Landing runs tend to be in the 2,500-3,000ft range because of the aircraft's clean profile and lack of drag parachute. They can be reduced by cutting the engine just prior to touchdown as its high idling speed produces significant thrust even with bleed valves open.

'If determining the landing speed of the airplane is a science rather than an art, balancing the airplane for landing is an art rather than a science', explained Steve Randle. Apart from its small, 70in, seldom-folded tip sections, the entire wing holds fuel. Its vast span and the minimal undercarriage make a finely-balanced fuel load essential. During a mission, the inboard tanks are used first, via sump tanks. This ensures that fuel remains in the outer wings to dampen torsional and bending forces on the structure. On the downwind leg the pilot slows the aircraft to a little above 'T-speed' and judges the balance situation purely by feel. Without risking a stall he aims for the slowest practicable speed, as the weight of the remaining fuel will be more apparent when aerodynamic lift forces are reduced. Fuel can then be transferred from the 'heavy' to the 'light' wing by operating the pumps. This too requires full attention, despite other pressing cockpit jobs, in case the imbalance is merely reversed, necessitating a missed approach and another circuit. The process is unaffected by the presence of Superpods on the wings. In 1987 the TR-1 squadron has found that it has more time to work on these techniques at its leisure since the departure of the 10th TRW's RF-4Cs, which previously vied for space in the circuit. However, the announcement that the base is to have two of the 81st TFW's busy A-10A squadrons cannot bring much cheer to the 95th RS crew-room.

As the aircraft approaches the runway the 'mobile' team prepares for action once again: the 'mobile' pilot is usually the one who started off the mission. The TR-1 sheds altitude reluctantly as it heads for the tarmac. Concentration on the runway centreline reduces the risk of drift and consequent damage. However, the process is not as difficult as it was in the U-2A/C era. Steve Randle again:

'At lower altitudes the airplane comes down pretty much like a normal airplane. We fly standard glidescope for landing. Really, the major difference between landing our airplane and any other is in the last 2-3ft above the runway. We have to stall the airplane in the air in order to make it stay on the ground. Any other airplane you can fly on to the runway; ours, you stall on to the runway. If you stall from more than about 3ft there is a great possibility of incurring structural damage. If you misjudge and don't stall, the main gear will hit the runway and then, since you're not

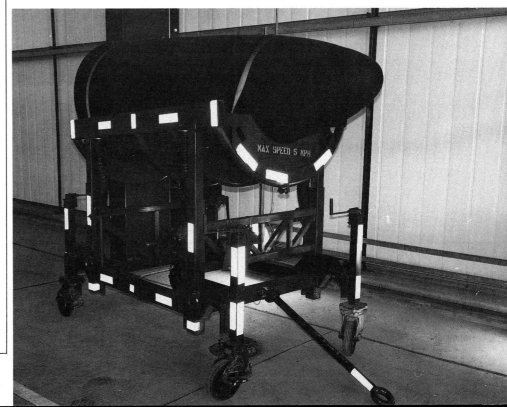

Above:
A Photint-equipped Dragon Lady, an unusual payload for the TR-1A which more typically works with synthetic aperture radar and Elint sensors.
Lockheed

Right:
An operational Superpod payload aboard TR-1A 80-1086 at Alconbury. This package is believed to comprise infra-red electro-optics and Elint equipment. *Authors*

Below:
The 'suitcase' payload aboard TR-1A 80-1086. The iron-ball black paint hides the Superpod's inner secrets. *Authors*

out of flying speed, the beast will bound back into the air. If it bounds more than 3 or 4ft, it will then stall and risk damage. It's very critical and that's why we have a mobile officer in a chase car calling off altitude. On the stall, the tail will settle on to the runway, followed rapidly by the main gear'. This time-honoured technique dates back to Tony Le Vier's adventurous landing of Article 341 at Groom Lake in 1955.

Cross-winds are a particular hazard during landing as the TR-1A can easily 'weathercock' at lower speeds. A 15kt cross-wind limit is standard for the 95th RS. In case of sudden windspeed increases during the landing phase the aircraft needs careful handling. Aileron control is obviously limited at near-stall speeds near the runway because of the wide span. In extreme conditions a wingtip may have to be deliberately 'dragged' to inhibit weathercocking, which, as Bob Uebelacker suggested, can be 'a dramatic sight during a night landing, generating a magnificent shower of sparks!' Abradable skid buttons are built into each wingtip skid to take the friction, replaced after an average of 100 landings. In favourable wind conditions, with good fuel-balancing, pilots attempt to keep the aircraft level as long as possible, aiming to reach almost zero speed before a wingtip touches down. The popular vision of super-fit road-runner ground crew chasing the Lady with pogo wheels in hand ready to jam them into the wing sockets while she is still trundling to a halt is another U-2 fallacy. However, pilots do take a pride in trying to stay level, even to the extent of running a rating system of points for each landing. Fuel balance is tested as part of this: 'We measure this in terms of crew chiefs — how many crew chiefs it takes to hold down the "light" wing. One crew-chief balance is very reasonable. Two crew chiefs is pretty gross, and if you have two crew chiefs and the "mobile" officer out of his car also jump on the wing, that probably calls for a round of beers someplace!'

Once the pogos are locked in place the engine is spooled up again and the TR-1A begins the run back to her hangar. Pilots exit the aircraft as early as possible in the shut-down procedure leaving post-flight checks to the 'mobile'. Release from the suit, a gradual return of normal bodily sensations and a lengthy de-briefing follow. A pilot can then relax in the Squadron HQ, surrounded by mementos of a history extending back to

1917 when, as the 95th Aero Squadron, the unit included pilots like Raoul Lufbery in its ranks. There will be no high-altitude flight for at least 48 hours for any returning flyer.

Sensors
Basic TR-1A fly-away cost in FY 1983 dollars was calculated at $17.1 million by the Air Force, though this excludes ECM, mission equipment, support equipment and spares, which, when lumped together, effectively turn the Black Lady into a $35 million airplane! The comparative simplicity of the aluminium structure (though Lockheed is experimenting with the use of advanced composites for rudders, elevators and airbrakes for improved performance) belies the sophistication of the aircraft's mission systems — the raison d'être of the beast. The pilots are, quite naturally, very shy about discussing Dragon Lady payloads, and for security reasons the authors were unable to ascertain the range of recon suites used on operational missions, which remain strictly classified. But such an investigation, as Steve Randle pointed out, would prove to be a bottomless pit: 'There are so many combinations, probably almost endless. It's not quite so bad if you're talking strictly TR-1 as opposed to U-2R: but even then, it seems that the aircraft are sprouting new antennas every time I turn around. As far as combinations of mission equipment is concerned, it's incredible!'. Suffice it to say that the potential integrated payloads of up to two tons are primarily sideways-looking or -listening, employed at high altitude at a distance away from the FEBA, as Bob put it, 'commensurate with the threat to the aircraft', while flying an autopilot-assisted parallel coverage or racetrack flight pattern. Payloads comprise systems from the four main categories of surveillance plus ancillary duties: peeping, prodding, hearsay and relay.

Photint peeping apparatus embodies two forms of equipment: hot-on-cold, temperature variation-sensitive infra-red scanners, plus long-range, electro-optic 6-110in focal length cameras. These passive devices are carried in the nose, Q-Bay or Superpods, for vertical wide-angle or oblique operation. As a rule of thumb, dedicated IR sensor fittings are denoted by zinc sulphide-type, thermally transparent reddish-brown panes in the nose or Superpods, and cameras by optically clear, bulbous glass oriels mounted in the Q-Bay —

though snapshot work is very much the province of the U-2R rather than TR-1A because of cameras' inherent limited-weather capability, better suited to monitoring movement in, say, the Persian Gulf or Central America, rather than weather-battered, cotton-covered Europe. IR sensors, on the other hand, are much more commonplace.

Like the majority of TR-1A sensors, 'look' gear works in real-time. Bob Uebelacker corrected the authors: 'Near real-time. In Vietnam it took four hours or so to get the data to the battle commanders. Today, all of USAFE works in near real-time. That means the information gets to the people who need it pretty quick — not an instantaneous picture of the battle area for commanders to peruse over while it's going on, but in a matter of minutes.' The mobility of modern Soviet forces dictates what is officially described as 'The rapid collection and dissemination of timely intelligence into the netted command, control, communications and intelligence [C^{3}I] network'. It's no good knowing what happened; the name of the game is 'what's happening?'. Certain specially-equipped members of USAFE's RF-4C community can furnish near real-time recce products in less than a quarter-of-an-hour of target coverage; presumably the 'Kickers' can perform the job at least as fast, and a considerable $240 million has been invested in Dragon Lady-related ground stations since 1982 with this in mind. To provide near real-time EO (electro-optic) coverage the sensors are tied to photoconductive or charged coupled devices, able to convert the raw imagery into coded signal format for near-instant relay back to ground, via data-link. There is no need — and no time for processing — huge magazines of celluloid in the fast-moving USAFE environment. This is what makes the TR-1 mission so different from that of the U-2R; 'customers' for the latter's data are often able to wait for superior celluloid-based intelligence a few hours later. Modes of operation and models of Photint equipment is shrouded in secrecy, but doubtless CAI Recon Optical, Honeywell, Texas Instruments and the Control Data Corp are heavily involved in the programme, all four firms having invested a considerable amount of effort in electro-optic sensors in recent years. Fitting the equipment into aerodynamically-compatible pallets is the responsibility of the sub-contractors, USAF

Logistics Command and Lockheed at Palmdale, California. Site 2 is constantly at work engineering new families of modular strap-ons and alternative fuselage panels. Lockheed tech-reps at Alconbury and Beale supervise installations during major configuration changes.

Prodding involves the use of active radar energy, scanned out from a dual planar array (two dishes mounted back-to-back) in a sideways-looking mode from the nose, either left or right, to quite literally probe, feel out and map the terrain and any enemy hardware. The most advanced of all these packages, originating from the AN/UPD-X, is the Hughes Advanced Synthetic Aperture Radar System (ASARS-2), first evaluated on U-2R 68-10336, and now operational on the TR-1A. ASARS-2 Dragon Ladies are easily distinguished by their more bulbous and blistered nose, 3ft longer than the standard slick fitting, though the only official statements available on the subject are a pair of recent Hughes news bulletins. Cleared for release in 1986: 'A new-generation mapping radar helps classify military targets automatically, even at extreme ranges.

The ASARS-2, designed to complement electro-optic sensors, is flown on a TR-1 reconnaissance aircraft and provides real-time radar imagery to a ground station in all weather. ASARS-2 sees with the high resolution of an infra-red sensor, but not from a perspective view. Instead, imagery is processed to show targets in an overhead view. One benefit of this approach is that a computer can more easily classify targets based on their outlines. The Air Force gave ASARS-2 an excellent rating after strict operational performance tests. Hughes is producing the system under a development and production contract'. And 1987: 'The first of a new generation of high-altitude

reconnaissance systems has been installed in a USAF TR-1 aircraft. The ASARS-2 provides high-resolution radar ground maps in real-time, in all types of weather. It produces long-range images superior to those delivered by photographic techniques. The unit's two side-looking antennas and the rest of the radar system, except for the cockpit displays, are mounted in a removable nose section. This allows the TR-1 aircraft's mission to be easily and rapidly changed by simply replacing the entire nose section. Hughes Aircraft Company developed ASARS-2 for the USAF'. A brief insight into the generically similar Loral (formerly Goodyear-Arizona) AN/APD-10, used by NASA U-2s and numerous 'Photo-Phantoms', helps cast some light on this shrouded subject.

The invention of synthetic aperture radar (SAR) is credited to scientist Carl Wiley who developed the new technique while working for Loral and who then went on to fine-tune his efforts at the USAF research division at Wright-Patterson AFB, Ohio. Previous sideways-looking airborne radar systems produced poor quality

images. This was simply because to get really good, crisp images, it was necessary to carry a huge antenna aloft — beam width being inversely proportional to antenna size and the sharper the beam, the sharper the reconnaissance product. SAR works this way artificially, by building up a picture using a series of neat, rapid sweeps. Correlator-processor equipment is employed to combine the returning signals into a continuous high-resolution image and convert the same into digital format for transmission back to ground, for decoding back into photo-quality radar images using a companion, ground-based correlator-processor. The Loral UPD SARs work at ranges of over 30nm from the target area, and cover a swathe 10nm wide. Working at altitude, ASARS-2 can cover an equal amount of territory at up to 70nm, can be pointed at any angle relative to the flight path not just 90° abeam and can detect both fixed and moving targets. In addition to the superb quality and immediacy of the pictures, ASARS-2 has other benefits: imagery can be collected at any time, regardless of weather, and is presented in an overview manner,

as if the TR-1A had dared to pass right over the target area! Cameras require less than 5/8th cloud and cannot see through camouflage or smoke, while infra-red sensors are at peak efficiency at night only; and both, when used in a stand-off manner, introduce perspective, making it very time-consuming for the intelligence people to identify and classify targets. The Loral AN/APD-10 SAR works at a constant scale of 1/100,000 across and along the imagery, and Hughes' ASARS-2 is probably no different. Magnification of images by a factor of up to 50 times — on TV (soft copy) or on print (hard copy) format — provides resolution of 3m, permitting rapid identification of enemy hardware ranging in size from individual tanks to entire Red Army battalions on the move. Moreover, by comparing old film strips to the latest imagery of a given piece of real estate, the ground-based interpretation computers can identify areas of interest automatically. New features in the fresh strip can be brought to the operator's attention in minutes, and classification performed automatically based on target signature, thus permitting in-flight redirection of

the TR-1A and its sensors for optimum target coverage. Spot coverage of such high-interest areas is available, apparently, at the flick of a switch. Survey data in turn is channelled to command centres where the battle area is viewed in vivid graphics on the monitor screen, laced with such vital data as UTM, Loran and Lat/Long co-ordinates. Within minutes of the start of a TR-1A ASARS-2 pass, Army commanders can be firing artillery or missiles at choice targets, and Air Force planners 'fragging' strike aircraft to stop mobile forces in their tracks.

Some reports have suggested that two ASARS-2 aircraft remain on standby *alert* at Alconbury. ASARS-2-configured jets there are, but the down-time necessary for mission planning and suiting-up precludes alert, and the long loiter capability of the TR-1A makes it unnecessary. Steve Randle: 'I can make the general comment that we don't have, nor do I ever envisage us having, an alert mission commitment'. With an eventual complement of over a dozen Dragon Ladies, supplemented during emergencies by aircraft flown over from Beale, it would be a relatively

simple matter for the 'Kickers' to maintain a brace of ASARS-2 jets on station at any one time, for vital round-the-clock target area surveillance.

Electronic hearsay — Elint, Comint and Sigint — provides timely intelligence on the enemy C^3 and radar network. Dragon Ladies configured for this role are usually denoted by 'farms' of 'Swiss Knife'-like blade and hook antennae on the Superpods and ventral fuselage, and by pinched, flat-sided noses containing phased-array antenna receivers. The lower frequency receivers, the 'farms', pick up signals and voice communications, which, after interception, can be used for one or more of three things: to cue infra-red or ASARS-2 sensors to areas of enemy activity right there and then; or, suitably decoded and translated by SAC intelligence and ESC, to ascertain the enemy's intentions and to help the friendly C^3-countermeasures (C^3/CM) community exploit weaknesses in the opposition's chain of command. Dedicated comm-jam aircraft can then be called on to throw the rigid system into chaos — such being the function of another Lockheed product, the EC-130H 'Compass Call' C^3/CM platform, a specialised variant of the 'Herky Bird' configured with a number of extremely powerful internally-mounted jammers and rear-end 'soccer net' of communications-receiving equipment. The American National Security Agency also enjoys access to Comint,

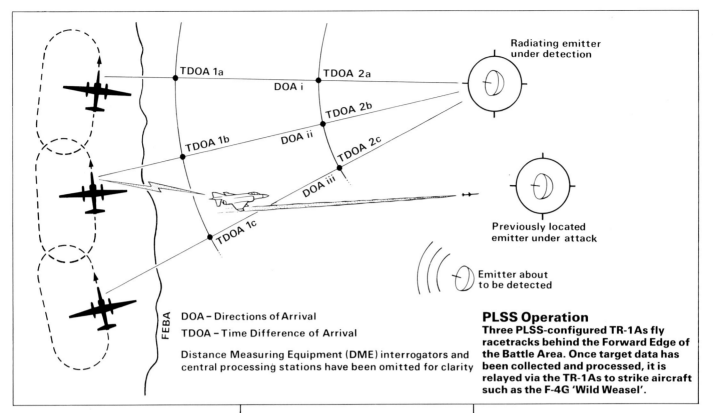

TDOA 1a

TDOA 2a

DOA i

TDOA 2b

TDOA 1b

DOA ii

TDOA 2c

DOA iii

TDOA 1c

TDOA 1c

Radiating emitter
under detection

Previously located
emitter under attack

Emitter about
to be detected

FEBA

DOA – Directions of Arrival

TDOA – Time Difference of Arrival

Distance Measuring Equipment (DME) interrogators and
central processing stations have been omitted for clarity

PLSS Operation
Three PLSS-configured TR-1As fly
racetracks behind the Forward Edge of
the Battle Area. Once target data has
been collected and processed, it is
relayed via the TR-1As to strike aircraft
such as the F-4G 'Wild Weasel'.

Above left:
**October 1985: TR-1A 80-1077 trundles
along the runway with an impressive
payload comprising ASARS-2,
sideways-looking infra-red, plus 'farms'
of intelligence and data-link antennae.**
Peter R. Foster

Left:
**An unusual sight of three TR-1As at
Beale. The middle aircraft is configured
with the Lockheed Space & Missile Co's
PLSS. Note the mini 'suitcase' bumps on
the aircraft's Superpods associated
with the DME equipment, and the
longer, flat-sided nose, which contains
the phased-array receivers.** *USAF*

in any shape or form, particularly
from the U-2R.

The phased-array receivers work in
the higher range of the spectrum, to
seek out and locate hostile emitters,
and monitor their mode of operation.
This Elint information, processed by
the SAC intell and ESC, assists in
providing jamming strategies and
protective measures for friendly
fighter-bombers' programmable
Radar Warning Receivers (RWRs) and
ECM, and the TR-1A's own RWR, ECM
and payload Electronic Counter-
Countermeasures (ECCM). Most such
Elint systems are believed to be
supplied by E-Systems and Litton-
Amecom, the latter manufacturer of
the similar AN/ALQ-125 TEREC tactical electromagnetic sensor which
equips two dozen USAF RF-4Cs.
TEREC can provide full details on
hostile emitters in one of two modes:
auto search, which can handle five of
10 in-flight selectable enemy radar
types in near real-time, and full

spectrum search, which maps the
enemy's complete EOB on tape for
analysis after aircraft recovery. No
doubt TR-1A Elint sensors can perform equally well but, like TEREC, are
subject to one major drawback: if it
proves necessary to fix the emitter
site as opposed to merely analysing
its mode of operation, a series of
Directions Of Arrival (DOAs) must be
taken as the aircraft flies along its
track so that the radar's position can
be triangulated, based on matching
the DOAs with relative aircraft
position. What this boils down to is
that the enemy must continue trans-
mitting long enough for sufficient
number of DOAs to be received.
Soviet-trained radar operators are
well aware of the dangers of staying
on the air for more than 10-15sec at a
time, and can foil systems like
TEREC: by simply reverting to
dummy load after a short burst (and
using several radars tied in together
to get a fuller picture), the emitter can
quickly dissolve into the electronic
backscatter. But this should have
been no countermeasure against the
TR-1A's newest and most advanced
Elint sensor: the Lockheed Space &
Missile Co's Precision Location Strike
System (PLSS)/Signal Location &
Targeting System (SLATS).

PLSS has had an agonisingly long
gestation period of some 15 years.
Started as a spin-off from the Pave
Onyx effort which aimed to field an
all-weather SA-2 SAM detector in
time for operations over North Vietnam (and which ultimately led to

TEREC in the postwar years), and
later funded as part of USAF's Pave
Strike defence-suppression initiative,
PLSS has seen successive prototype
forms during stop-go financing.
Originally developed by IBM as the
Advanced Location Strike System
(ALSS), in 1987 Lockheed's subsequent PLSS looked set to go into
service, with tests to continue for
some time as part of a follow-on $15
million RDT&E (Research, Development, Test and Engineering) effort.
However, in early 1988 it was
announced that the system's development would be curtailed because
of follow-up funding restrictions,
though a standby contingency force
will remain at Beale, ready for
possible wartime deployment, using
equipment already funded.

TR-1As configured for the job wear
a kit comprising Harris Corp Superpod attachments complete with Distance Measuring Equipment (DME)
interrogators, and an elongated,
pinched nose containing twin
phased-array receivers supplied by
E-Systems, for left or right coverage.
The Control Data Corp and Sperry are
also involved as sub-contractors to
Lockheed, handling data-link.

Three PLSS-configured TR-1As
flying racetrack behind the FEBA —
the 'airborne mission sub-systems' —
compare, between them, the incoming *Time Difference* Of Arrival
(TDOAs) of enemy radar emissions,
correlated with an onboard atomic
clock for chronological precision; this
enables their companion ground-

based central processing UYK-25 PLSS computers — to which they are data-linked — to pinpoint enemy radar sites and C^3 installations using a form of 'inverse Loran', as the DoD has euphemistically described the technique, in a matter of seconds. To assist the central processing station sort out the wheat from the chaff amidst the millions of pulses on the airwaves, approximate DOAs are also supplied, along with precise TR-1 positions based on DME interrogation between the Black Ladies and pre-positioned battery-operated DME transponders located at pre-surveyed sites in the field. Once a target has been located, the central processing station relays the target data back via the TR-1As in an up-link mode to suitably-equipped strike and support aircraft or their DME-assisted, remote-control weapons. Aircraft and weaponry geared to fit into the PLSS scheme of things include the F-4G 'Wild Weasel' Phantoms and their stand-off AGM-88 HARM anti-radar missiles, and GBU-15/AGM-130-toting F-4Es and F-111s, whose data-linked electro-optically-guided Rockwell bombs can be similarly 'flown' to the target area by the ground station. (Final corrections to target lock-on for pinpoint accuracy can be effected by the strike crews, employing Hughes AN/AXQ-14 data-links of their own to acquire video communication with the bombs' seekers to put the cross-hairs smack on target, just prior to bomb impact.) The net result is that enemy anti-air defences can be suppressed without the strike forces ever having to come into line of sight with the target emitters, which in turn can be plotted accurately on the basis of a short burst. ALSS radar-fixing accuracy during tests held at White Sands Missile Range in 1972 was sufficiently good to help put ten 2,000lb DME-assisted Mk 84 bombs within an average of 75ft of the target dishes; with the latest generation of very high-speed integrated circuits and microprocessing electronics and strike weapons with smart terminal guidance or reversionary TV modes, PLSS can better that figure substantially, while handling a much larger and more bewildering array of threats, along a whole front.

Doubts have been expressed from some quarters concerning the effects that Soviet jamming and decoy emitters may have on the tactical efficacy of the system. In South-East Asia, Robert McNamara's billion-dollar brainchild, the 'Igloo White' electronic network (designed to pick up movement along the Ho Chi Minh Trail), was easily foiled by cunning Vietnamese peasants. 'People sniffers' were activated by carefully placed bags of buffalo urine and a well-aimed string of rocket or mortar rounds triggered off ADSID acoustic sensors, diverting swarms of B-52s, Gunships, Intruders and Phantoms away from the truck convoys. But PLSS fights a pure electronic battle, and ECCM is extensive. The final proof of the pudding came in March and April 1987, when PLSS successfully completed a series of very stringent trials at Nellis TFWC, Nevada, during a mock electronic combat 'Green Flag' effort, pinpointing emitters to within a few feet and demonstrating its ability to divert the 'Wild Weasel' radar-killers on to prime electronic installations, despite extensive jamming and decoy interference. PLSS was due to come to Alconbury for operational trials in the USAFE environment in 1988, but early in 1988 it was reported that the Pentagon had been unable to come up with around $50 million in the FY88 budget for an European demonstration programme.

Relay is an integral part of TR-1A operations. Not only is all work performed in near real-time, requiring high-priority intelligence to be data-linked back to ground for immediate processing, but urgent instructions from ground centres to strike and support aircraft out of line of sight to the command posts must be conveyed via TR-1A. The Dragon Lady's super-loiter capability at high altitude makes it a prime candidate for this task. One can also envisage a scenario in which critical communications satellites are knocked out, forcing a number of TR-1As to remain airborne as relay ships in conjunction with SAC's EC-135s — and possibly in a chain stretching the Atlantic Ocean, keeping the red telephone operational in Washington!

Future assignments

More jobs are envisaged and the USAF claims that 'Stated mission requirements justify 37 aircraft'; funding for additional TR-1 and U-2R sensors continues also, with $80.4 million earmarked in FY88 for procurement and RDT&E, and another $118.8 million requested for FY89 — an ongoing, sizeable investment which underlines the priority status of the Dragon Lady even 30 years after its inception.

The role the USAF would have liked to see the TR-1A perform was that of airborne moving target locator, utilising radar to locate mobile enemy armoured forces and then direct strike traffic on to the opposition without the need for them to pop-up into the tough SAM and AAA defences — an anti-tank version of PLSS. Developed originally under DARPA's Pave Mover and 'Assault Breaker' programmes, the USAF and US Army eventually merged the concept under the acronym J-STARS (otherwise known as the joint surveillance & target attack radar system). After months of gnashing of teeth the USAF capitulated to the Army's demands that the J-STARS target locator should carry some of their personnel aboard and the TR-1 was dropped; instead, purpose-built EC-18s (based on the Navy E-6, a military production derivative of the Boeing 707), is scheduled to carry the package operationally. The controversial aircraft is expected to achieve IOC in the early 1990s.

Another TR-1A role which the USAF is still toying with is that of a mini-AWACS platform. Lockheed has developed a 14ft-long, 4ft-wide, 3ft-deep inflatable Kevlar radome of negligible weight which billows out from under the fuselage after take-off, to permit scanner operation. The aircraft has undergone tests in the western United States and officials, by all accounts, were impressed with the preliminary findings: the TR-1A's high-flying abilities not only offer excellent coverage with a modest antenna, but also much reduced vulnerability to enemy MiGs — one of the major criticisms levied by Congress's General Accounting Office against the big Boeing E-3A AWACS early on in that particular programme. TR-1A AWACS is up for grabs.

The TR-1 mission will inevitably extend into further realms of weird and wonderful peeping, prodding, hearsay and relay work as the needs arise and the technology emerges. Certainly, the Dragon Lady community can look forward to a long, exciting and prosperous career; and at the forefront is Alconbury's 95th RS, 17th RW, whose Wing motto sums up the adventurousness of the high-flyers: 'Toujours Au Danger'. And would the pilots like to have a break and do a tour in the F-15, allegedly *the* ultimate USAF fighter? Dragon Lady handling requires much more experienced talents and the pilots resounded with a unanimous 'No!'

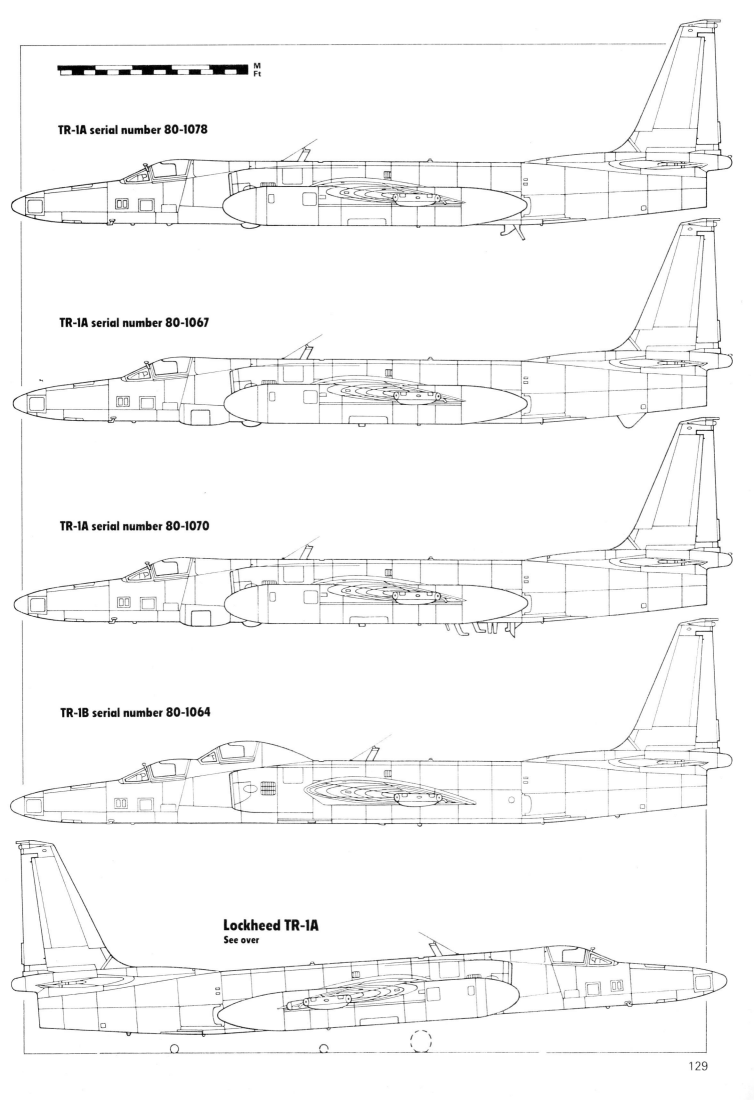

TR-1A serial number 80-1078

TR-1A serial number 80-1067

TR-1A serial number 80-1070

TR-1B serial number 80-1064

Lockheed TR-1A
See over

M
Ft

Lockheed TR-1A
Serial numbers 80-1066, 80-1067, 80-1068 and 80-1069

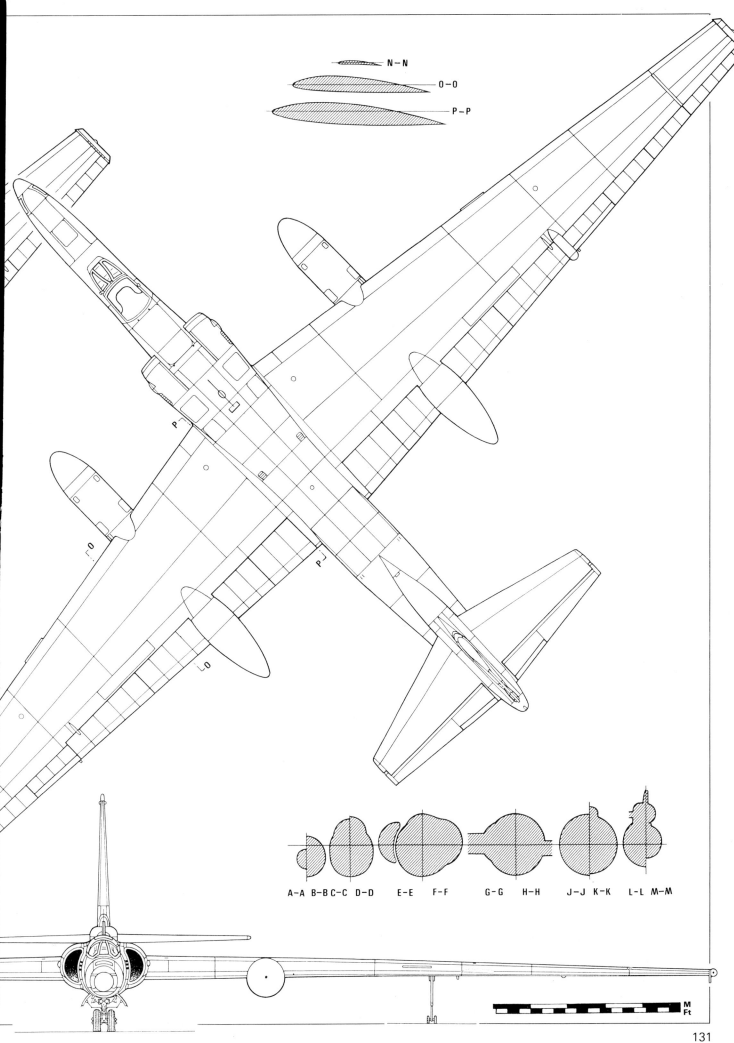

N—N

O—O

P—P

A-A B-B C-C D-D   E-E   F-F   G-G   H-H   J-J K-K   L-L M-M

M
Ft

7
White Angels from Ames

NASA captured the hearts and minds of people across the globe with its Mercury, Gemini and Apollo space-shots of the 1960s, culminating in man's first step on the Moon in July 1969. In the 1970s NASA progressed on to moon-roaming, Skylab, Apollo-Soyuz and unmanned Viking, Pioneer and Voyager probes to Mars and the outer Solar System, and the 1980s heralded the dawn of the reusable space vehicle; Shuttle, which in the tragic aftermath of the *Challenger* accident is licking its wounds in preparation for a new, revitalised launch schedule.

Less well known is NASA's far broader and often wider-reaching exploits in pushing the boundaries in such diverse fields of aeronautics as metallurgy, aerodynamics, thermo-dynamics and propulsion: and their equally tireless investigation of the structure and resources of our own planet. To assist this research, NASA (formerly the National Advisory Committee for Aeronautics, NACA) oper-ates a number of special labs at 10 installations scattered across the USA, six of which maintain compara-tively large fleets of aircraft. At the forefront is NASA's Ames Research

Laboratory located at Moffett Field NAS, California, which flies a mixed force of 20 predominantly ex-US service machines ranging in size and performance from the OH-6A 'Loach' to the C-141 Starlifter; of those, by far the most intriguing collection belongs to John Arvesen's select High Altitude Missions Branch, whose five NASA and Lockheed contract pilots fly a duo of Dragon Ladies — Ames' 'White Angels'.

The benefits to be reaped from operating a Federally-budgeted civil high-flying force are self-evident: the Lockheed White Ladies can see into

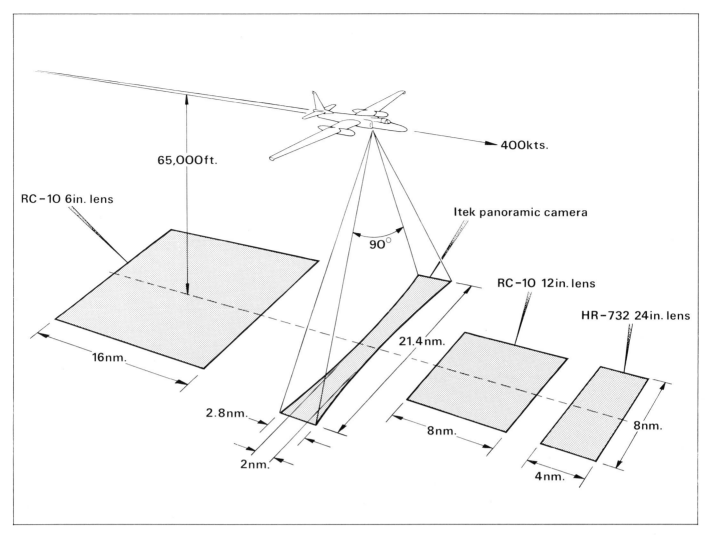

space without the protective atmospheric shell of the Earth to obscure imagery or deflect vital incoming, tell-tale matter from the heavens; they can grab 'particulate matter' trapped in the upper atmosphere where no other planes can reach; examine the movement and ratio of specific chemicals in the atmosphere and stratosphere such as ammonia, freon, methane, ozone and water; and in a downwards-looking mode can not only map wide tracts of our planet — oceans, icecaps and continents — but also observe violent meteorological phenomena with relative impunity up on their lofty and very stable perch.

The first true civilian White Dragons — U-2Cs N708NA/56-6681 and N709NA/56-6682,the seventh and eighth aircraft in the initial production lot — joined the team in 1971. Both aircraft had seen extensive service with SAC's 4080th SRW at the height

Left:
Ex-USAF U-2C 56-6682, NASA serial N709NA, being pre-flighted at Moffett Field with 'howdah' sunshade in place to keep the cockpit cool.
Lockheed via Tim Perry

High Altitude Camera Specifications — U-2/ER-2.

Designation	Lens (focal length/aperture)	Film format (in)	Ground coverage at 65,000ft	Nominal resolution at 65,000ft
Vinten (four)	1¾in/f2·8	70mm (2¼×2³⁄₁₆)	25·9km×25·9km (14nm×14nm) (each)	10-20m
I²S Multispectral (four bands) K-22	100mm/f2·8	9×9 (4 at 3·5)	16·7km×16·7km (9nm×9nm)	6-10m
RC-10	6in/f4	9×9	29·7km×29·7km (16nm×16nm)	3-8m
RC-10	12in/f4	9×9	14·8km×14·8km (8nm×8nm)	1·5-4m
HR-732	24in/f8	9×18	7·4km×14·8km (4nm×8nm)	0·6-3m
HR-73B-1	36in/f10	18×18	9·8km×9·8km (5·3nm×5·3nm)	0·5-2m
Itek Panoramic (Optical Bar)	24in/f3·5	4·5×35in (90°) to 4·5×60in (140°)	3·7km×39·6km (2nm×21·4nm) 3·7km×109km (2nm×58·7nm)	0·3-2m
Research Camera	24in/f3·5	2¼×30	2km×20km (1·1nm×11nm) useable	0·1-1m

of the Cuban missile crisis, then went on to perform carrier trials aboard the USS *Enterprise* before being reassigned to NASA for a gentler but no less challenging flight programme. Flying missions similar to those performed by a trio of NASA/ Martin RB-57Fs (which flew from Ellington ANGB, Texas, under the authority of the Lyndon B. Johnson Space Center headquartered at Houston) and a duo of USAF U-2Ds

(employed by the Edwards AFFTC 6512th Test Squadron), the aircraft probed several little-known aspects of meteorology, including clear air turbulence (during the CAT and HICAT missions), storm research (Project 'Rough Rider'), along with flood and volcanic ash disaster damage assessment and a host of other tasks to meet the seemingly insatiable appetites of the US Departments of Agriculture and Water and

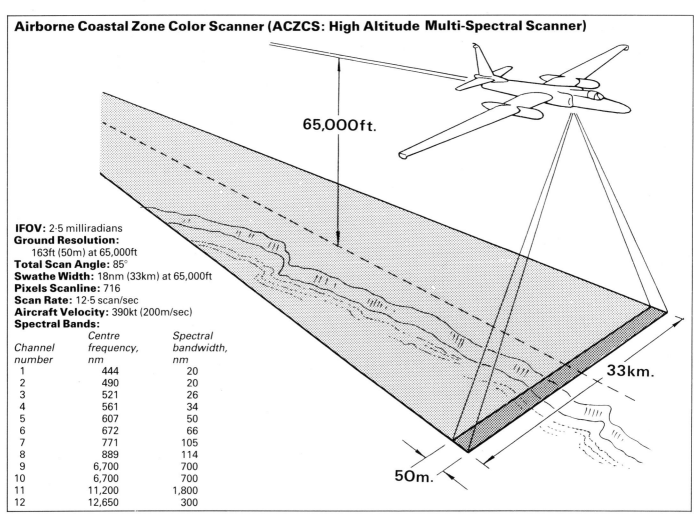

Airborne Coastal Zone Color Scanner (ACZCS: High Altitude Multi-Spectral Scanner)

65,000ft.

IFOV: 2·5 milliradians
Ground Resolution:
  163ft (50m) at 65,000ft
Total Scan Angle: 85°
Swathe Width: 18nm (33km) at 65,000ft
Pixels Scanline: 716
Scan Rate: 12·5 scan/sec
Aircraft Velocity: 390kt (200m/sec)
Spectral Bands:

Channel number	Centre frequency, nm	Spectral bandwidth, nm
1	444	20
2	490	20
3	521	26
4	561	34
5	607	50
6	672	66
7	771	105
8	889	114
9	6,700	700
10	6,700	700
11	11,200	1,800
12	12,650	300

33km.

50m.

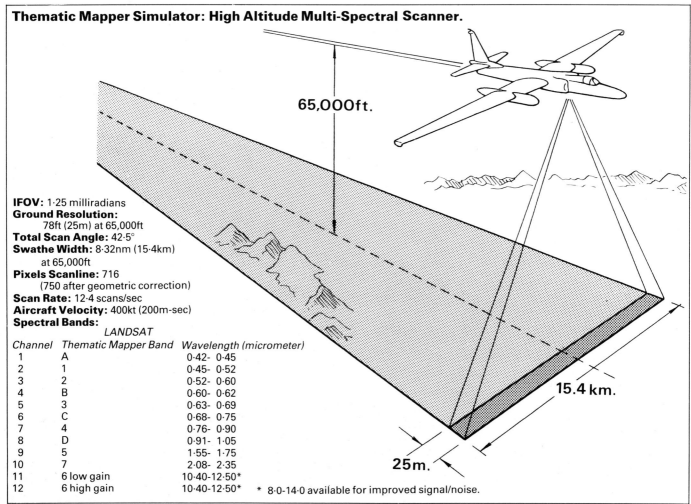

Thematic Mapper Simulator: High Altitude Multi-Spectral Scanner.

65,000ft.

IFOV: 1·25 milliradians
Ground Resolution:
  78ft (25m) at 65,000ft
Total Scan Angle: 42·5°
Swathe Width: 8·32nm (15·4km)
  at 65,000ft
Pixels Scanline: 716
  (750 after geometric correction)
Scan Rate: 12·4 scans/sec
Aircraft Velocity: 400kt (200m-sec)
Spectral Bands:

Channel	LANDSAT Thematic Mapper Band	Wavelength (micrometer)
1	A	0·42- 0·45
2	1	0·45- 0·52
3	2	0·52- 0·60
4	B	0·60- 0·62
5	3	0·63- 0·69
6	C	0·68- 0·75
7	4	0·76- 0·90
8	D	0·91- 1·05
9	5	1·55- 1·75
10	7	2·08- 2·35
11	6 low gain	10·40-12·50*
12	6 high gain	10·40-12·50*

* 8·0-14·0 available for improved signal/noise.

15.4 km.

25m.

Payload Areas

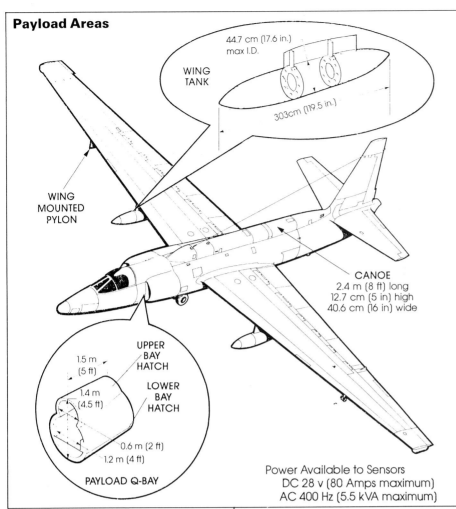

WING TANK
44.7 cm (17.6 in.) max I.D.
303cm (119.5 in.)

WING MOUNTED PYLON

CANOE
2.4 m (8 ft) long
12.7 cm (5 in) high
40.6 cm (16 in) wide

UPPER BAY HATCH
LOWER BAY HATCH
1.5 m (5 ft)
1.4 m (4.5 ft)
0.6 m (2 ft)
1.2 m (4 ft)
PAYLOAD Q-BAY

Power Available to Sensors
DC 28 v (80 Amps maximum)
AC 400 Hz (5.5 kVA maximum)

has just been retired and is slated to go on permanent display at Ames, while N709NA will be retired in the spring of 1989, and is scheduled to serve as a display piece at Robins AFB, Georgia.

In common with its forbears, the demilitarised ER-2 is not dissimilar from its black military sisters, built around the same engine, cockpit and Litton LTN-72RH INS. The main differences lie with the nav-comm equipment, Q-Bay and Superpod payloads, lack of threat warning and ECM gear, and the pristine gloss white and blue decor demarcated by pale blue stripes — though the aircraft wear their old USAF serial numbers on the airbrakes to avoid incurring Federal fuel taxes: a prudent business move. Operations, too, are by necessity very similar, with pilots obliged to wear a full

Below:
A drift-sight view of Mount St Helens, shot by Lockheed contract pilot Ronald W. Williams while flying N709NA at 65,000ft over the mountain range in Washington. The aircraft was flying at an indicated airspeed of 120kt. Note the digital co-ordinates displayed on the inertial navigation system. *Lockheed*

the Environmental Protection Agency. An important date was 10 June 1981, when the long-awaited Earth Resources-2 Dragon Lady, NASA N706NA/80-1063, arrived at the Ames facility piloted by Martin A. Knutson, chief of the Airborne Missions & Applications Division at Moffett Field. Flown for the first time on 11 May 1981, with Lockheed test pilot Art Peterson in charge, the bird flew its first NASA mission — a water resources sortie — on 12 June. The pilot response was one of excitement. The less forgiving nature of the U-2C had forced NASA to stay well clear of 'coffin corner' and optimise its pay-loads for operations at or below 65,000ft; it was with considerable envy that the Ames team viewed the bigger, higher-flying and longer-endurance U-2R for well on nigh a decade. The more tolerant ER-2 has expanded Ames' range of options considerably, and has been the major driving factor behind the recent retirement of the tired old RB-57Fs at Ellington, together with a commensurate reduction in U-2C sorties — the ER-2 has no less than 2·75 times the max payload capacity of the U-2C, and will shortly take over the job completely, when NASA receives its second ER-2 in March 1989. N708NA

NASA-Ames Research Center Stratospheric Sensor Platform

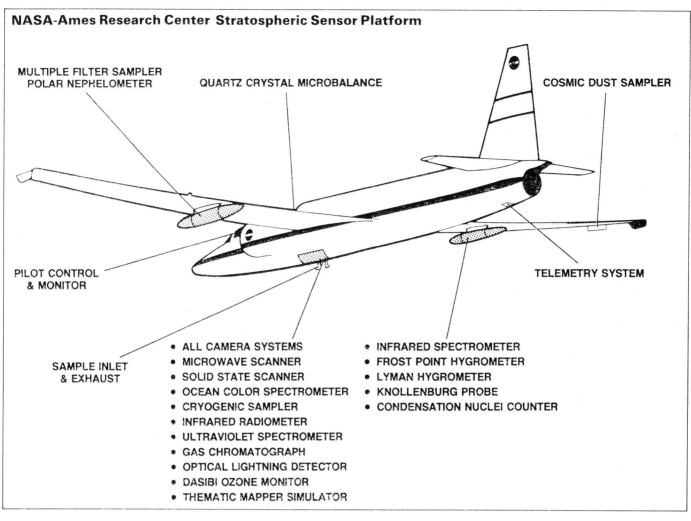

MULTIPLE FILTER SAMPLER
POLAR NEPHELOMETER

QUARTZ CRYSTAL MICROBALANCE

COSMIC DUST SAMPLER

PILOT CONTROL
& MONITOR

TELEMETRY SYSTEM

SAMPLE INLET
& EXHAUST

- ALL CAMERA SYSTEMS
- MICROWAVE SCANNER
- SOLID STATE SCANNER
- OCEAN COLOR SPECTROMETER
- CRYOGENIC SAMPLER
- INFRARED RADIOMETER
- ULTRAVIOLET SPECTROMETER
- GAS CHROMATOGRAPH
- OPTICAL LIGHTNING DETECTOR
- DASIBI OZONE MONITOR
- THEMATIC MAPPER SIMULATOR

- INFRARED SPECTROMETER
- FROST POINT HYGROMETER
- LYMAN HYGROMETER
- KNOLLENBURG PROBE
- CONDENSATION NUCLEI COUNTER

ER-2 Instrument Configuration for Antarctic Ozone Programme

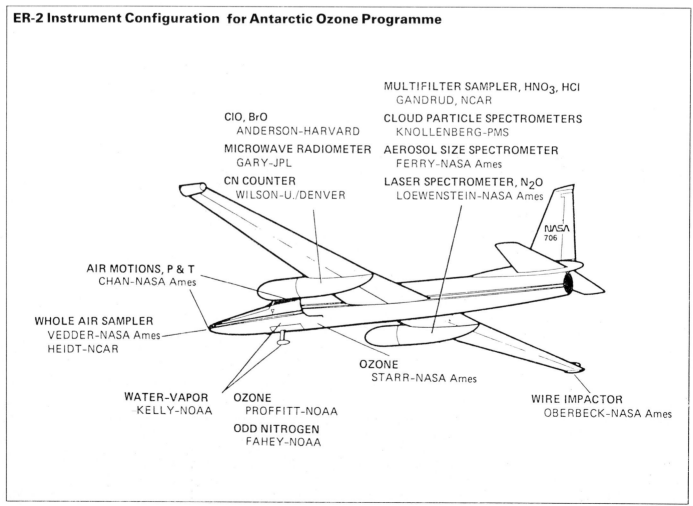

ClO, BrO
ANDERSON-HARVARD

MICROWAVE RADIOMETER
GARY-JPL

CN COUNTER
WILSON-U./DENVER

MULTIFILTER SAMPLER, HNO$_3$, HCl
GANDRUD, NCAR

CLOUD PARTICLE SPECTROMETERS
KNOLLENBERG-PMS

AEROSOL SIZE SPECTROMETER
FERRY-NASA Ames

LASER SPECTROMETER, N$_2$O
LOEWENSTEIN-NASA Ames

AIR MOTIONS, P & T
CHAN-NASA Ames

WHOLE AIR SAMPLER
VEDDER-NASA Ames
HEIDT-NCAR

OZONE
STARR-NASA Ames

WATER-VAPOR
KELLY-NOAA

OZONE
PROFFITT-NOAA

ODD NITROGEN
FAHEY-NOAA

WIRE IMPACTOR
OBERBECK-NASA Ames

Above:
Ames' U-2C No N708NA (ex-USAF U-2C 56-6681) soaring high above the ground. The sensor windows in the Q-Bay are worthy of note, as is the early 1970s decor and marking on the 'doghouse' which reads: 'NASA survey aircraft No 4'. *Lockheed*

pressure suit, and their entourage of physiological support, payload specialist and maintenance staff organised into a travelling party of 12-15 NASA and Lockheed personnel (the size of the team depending on the length and nature of the deployment) to cater for missions away from the home drome. Flights are flown around the clock, as required, and are typically of six hours' duration.

Most such sorties are flown within the boundaries of the Continental USA, though overseas assignments are not uncommon, often taking advantage of the resources available at USAF U-2R forward OLs, such as Mildenhall, England, which are better suited to the unique support demands of the aircraft; the South American and Australian continents have featured strongly as venues in recent years, too. US Federal Agencies and State Governments can actually rent a U-2C/ER-2 sortie from NASA's High Altitude Missions Branch (address available via the Editor!) for just about anything one may fancy — subject to references and formal NASA approval. For example, a wheat farmer who was having considerable difficulty proving to the US Department of Agricul-

ture that he was eligible for reimbursement under the latter's 'Payment in Kind Program' obtained a suitable photo of his homestead from NASA which resulted in a cheque for $20,000 slipping into his mailbox. High altitude metric and panoramic cameras of 6, 12 or 24in focal lengths are employed for this kind of work, supplied by Wild-Heerbrug and Itek, able to use the full range of colour, infra-red and black & white films available, along with multispectral scanner systems, the imagery from which may be computer-enhanced using an Interactive Digital Image Manipulation System (IDIMS) after processing, to highlight areas of interest.

Air sampling is another facility on offer. Environmental lobbyists and academic bodies are presently engaging NASA in ozone-level research, air-sampling fluorocarbons and hydrocarbons from the dreaded aerosol can, car and jet engine; and a few of Nature's own often more-dramatic ozone-destructive and rejuvinatory processes.

More commercially-oriented work is performed under special contracts. The potential success of satellite sensors may be pre-gauged from a high-flying White Angel before a

company or agency commits itself to a multi-million dollar rocket launch into orbit, giving them time to fine-tune their payloads, as has proved so successful with LANDSAT I-V camera and infra-red Earth resources sensors. NASA's own space-rocketing branch have a considerable vested interest in these simulations.

Ames' three angels have also been seeking answers to the ultimate question: 'the meaning of life, the Universe and everything', to quote a well known hitch-hikers' guide. Recent firsts have included the collection of 4·5 billion year-old intergalactic or cosmic dusts wafting into the Earth's upper atmosphere; and a March 1979 deployment to Lima, Peru, drew upon U-2C N708NA for a series of four night sorties for the

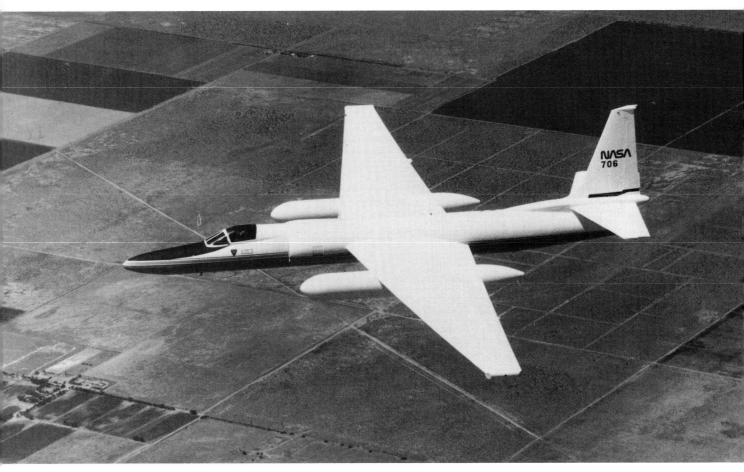

rather exotic measurement of the movement of the Earth and our Galaxy relative to intergalactic matter, using a Differential Microwave Radiometer to verify the 'Big Bang' theory. All very mind-boggling stuff!

Regarding more Earthly matters, NASA's U-2s are getting to grips with thematic-mapping sensors and more advanced imaging spectrometers such as the aptly named AVIRIS — the Airborne Visible/Infra-Red Imaging Spectrometer. AVIRIS measures reflected solar radiation from this planet's surface in 224 spectral bands to map wide areas in swathes 11km wide at a time with 20m resolution, to help detect the whereabouts of precious minerals and fossil fuels; for less economic gain it also delineates the plate tectonic structure of the Earth's crust, *inter alia*, to help geologists anticipate areas susceptible to earthquakes, avalanches, floods and volcanic activity — of vital importance to the Richter scale-monitoring community. Hundreds of other activities are performed to keep an eye on pollutants, and with water, agricultural and forest resource management in mind.

The work of the NASA hi-alt effort doubtless makes Clarence 'Kelly' Johnson as proud as do the efforts of his military offspring. Kelly in fact went so far as to reiterate some wise words from his autobiography *More Than My Share Of It All* on American TV, saying 'The best airplane . . . is going to be the crop-duster; it can feed us, keep us healthy and help save the country . . . '. NASA's White Angels go a long way towards achieving this, while also expanding man's knowledge of his immediate environment, and his place in the Universe as a whole. Ultimately, the human race will have to let go of mother Earth's apron strings and leave home — something with which we've toyed with our extraterrestrial 'weekend' excursions to the Moon, and remote-controlled exploration of the outer Solar System. The U-2 has contributed a great deal to our understanding of the complexities of star voyaging. Designed purely for military work, the high-flying big-wing has also become a magnificent tool of peace, and while we continue to live at home it enables us to make more efficient yet conscientious use of the finite resources of this planet.

And what of the other surveillance aircraft? The dwindling numbers of serviceable SR-71 Habus — the USAF is planning to cut the force by 50% to six aircraft, as an economy move — will doubtless be flying at the speed-o'-heat for several years yet, while the TR-1 and its older sister the U-2R may well be in demand for another 30 years. But their ultimate retirement will not mark the end of the Blackbirds story: the newly-formed Lockheed Aeronautical Systems Co is busy at work on USAF's successor to the F-15, the Advanced Tactical Fighter, while even more secret Lockheed stealth strike-surveillance aircraft such as the alleged F-19 Nightingale are believed to be operational in considerable numbers at the remote outpost at Groom Lake, Nevada. A whole new chapter has opened up.

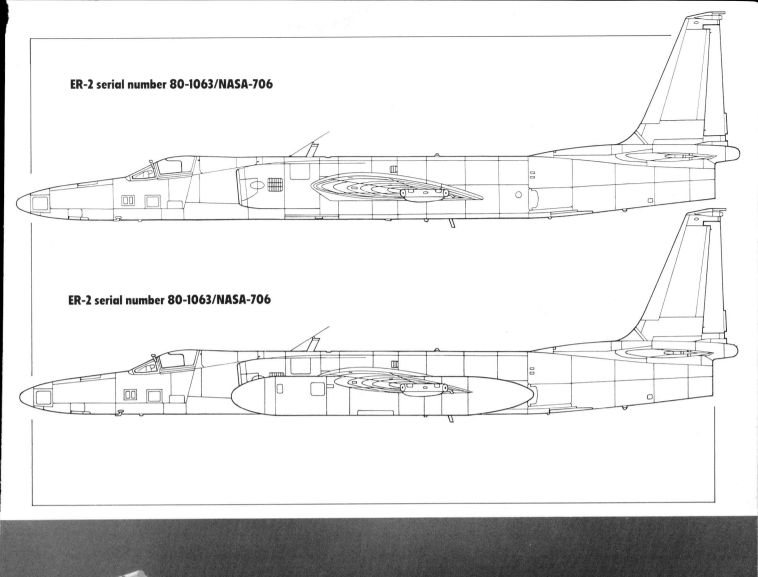

ER-2 serial number 80-1063/NASA-706

ER-2 serial number 80-1063/NASA-706

Appendices

1 Serial Numbers

Serial Numbers	Quantity	Model	Notes
56-6675-6722	48	U-2A-C	
6951-6955	5	U-2D	
60-6924-6933	10	A-12	
6934-6936	3	YF-12A	
6937-6941	5	A-12	06937 serial also used on SR-71A 17951 when transferred to NASA in July 1971 as a YF-12C. Not proceeded with.
6942-6948	7	A-12	
64-17950-17955	6	SR-71A	
17956-17957	2	SR-71B	
17958-137980	23	SR-71A	
17981	1	SR-71C	Conversion of YF-12 06934, post-accident.
17982-17984	3	SR-71A	Not proceeded with.
68-10329-10345	17	U-2R	
10346-10353	8	U-2R	Believed not proceeded with.
80-1063	1	ER-2	A second ER-2 is under construction.
1064-1065	2	TR-1B	
1066-1088+	23+	TR-1A	Production continues?

'FAA serials' N800X-N809X were used on U-2 aircraft during Lockheed rework or trials and for various CIA operational uses.

All aircraft were five-figure abbreviated serials: eg SR-71B 64-17956 bears the tail number 17956, and TR-1A 80-1086 the fin serial 01086.

The allocation of serials for most U-2s was deliberately confusing. Tail numbers have been changed frequently, re-allocated or re-used when aircraft were written off. No accurate assessment can be made until individual aircraft records are declassified in AD2011.

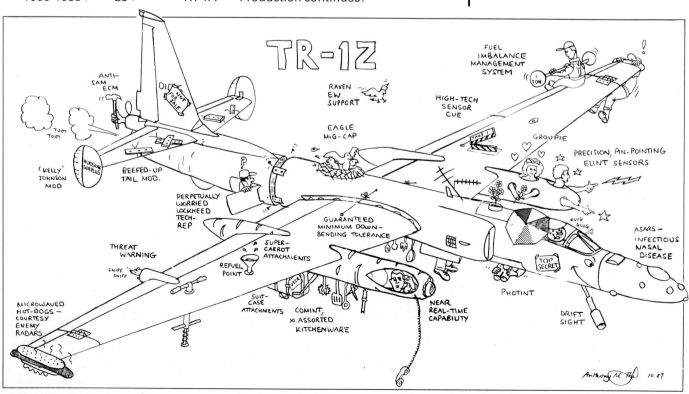

2 Specifications

	U-2A-G	U-2R/TR-1	A-12	F-12	SR-71A	D-21
Length (excluding pitots*) (ft)	49·75	62·9	98·75* 102	101·6* 105·2	103·8* 107·4	43·2
Span (ft)	80·2	103	55·6	55·6	55·6	17
Height (ft)	15·2	16·5	18·5	18·5	18·5	8
Wing area (sq ft)	600	1,000	1,795	1,795	1,795	?
Empty weight (lb)	12,000 (U-2A) up to 14,375 (U-2G	15,101	60,000	60,730	67,500	10,000?
Max take-off weight (lb)	22,100 (U-2A) up to 24,475 (U-2G	41,000	120,000	127,000	172,000	20,000?
Powerplant	J57 or J75-P-13A/B	J75-P-13B	2×J75 or J58	2×J58	2×J58	RJ43-MA-11 (and booster)
Crew	1 (or 2, U-2CT/D)	1 (2, TR-1B)	1 (2, 'Goose' birds)	2	2	0
'Red line' max cruise speed (Mach)	0·72	0·82	3·6	3·2	3·2	4+
Max operational ceiling (ft)	78,000 (U2A) 75,000 (U-2G)	78,500	95,000	85,000	85,000	100,000?
Unrefuelled range (miles)	4,750 (U-2A)	5,500	2,500	2,500	3,250	1,250?
Sensor payload (lb)	750 (U-2A, typical)	>3,000	3,000	3,300 (weapons)	3,500	<500?

Above:
N706NA thunders down the runway, with pogos secured in place. The large Superpods provide around 90cu ft of sensor space. Additional equipment may be carried in the nose, Q-Bay aft of the cockpit, and in the aft pressure cavity and tailcone, though the latter are not used by NASA. *Lockheed*

Left:
Lockheed Burbank's famous Blackbird duo in formation: SR-71 64-17955 (nicknamed 'The Flower') with the company's famous 'Skunk' symbol on its fins, and U-2R 68-10336, complete with Hughes ASARS-2 radar nose.
Lockheed

3 Records

YF-12 Records

1 May 1965	World and Class sustained altitude	USA	80,258ft
1 May 1965	World and Class speed record over a 15/25km closed course	USA	2,070mph
1 May 1965	World speed record over a 500km closed course	USA	1,643mph*
1 May 1965	World and Class speed record over a 1,000km closed course (captured same World and Class speed records with 1,000kg and 2,000kg payloads)	USA	1,689mph*

*Later captured by the USSR flying the E-266 (MiG-25) in October 1967.

SR-71 World Records

Official Absolute World Records, 31 December 1976
(Maximum performance in any class)

28 July 1976	Altitude in horizontal flight Capt Robert C. Helt, USAF	USA	25,929·031m 85,068·997ft
28 July 1976	Speed over a straight course Capt Eldon W. Joersz, USAF	USA	3,529·56km/h 2,193·167mph
27 July 1976	Speed over a closed circuit Maj Adolphus H. Bledsoe Jr, USAF	USA	3,367·221km/h 2,092·294mph

Class C-1, Group III (Jet) without payload

28 July 1976	Altitude in horizontal flight Capt Robert C. Helt, USAF	USA	25,929·031m 85,068·997ft
28 July 1976	Speed over a straight course Capt Eldon W. Joersz, USAF	USA	3,529·56km/h 2,193·167mph
27 July 1976	Closed circuit — 1,000km, Speed Maj Adolphus H. Bledsoe Jr, USAF	USA	3,367·221km/h 2,092·294mph

Class C-1, Group III (Jet) with 1,000kg payload

27 July 1976	Closed circuit — 1,000km Speed Maj Adolphus H. Bledsoe Jr, USAF	USA	3,367·221km/h 2,092·294mph

Class C-1, Group III (Jet)

1 September 1974	Speed over a recognised course — New York to London Maj James V. Sullivan, USAF	USA	2,908·026km/h 1,806·964mph
13 September 1974	Speed over a recognised course — London to Los Angeles Capt Harold B. Adams, USAF	USA	2,310·353km/h 1,435·587mph

Note: 9th SRW Habu crew Lieutenant Colonels Estes and Vick were awarded the Mackay Trophy for 1971 for a demonstration flight which covered 15,000 miles in 10½ hours — flying a loop over the United States from and back to California. This was equivalent to a non-stop flight from San Francisco to Paris and back!

Above right:
No less than eight A-12s are featured in this shot, huddled together at Lockheed-Palmdale. The silver and black A-12 at the back of the photo is the J75-powered, twin-seat 'Titanium Goose'. *Lockheed*

Left:
Record-setters (from left to right) Col Jim Coonie, Col Walt Daniel, Col 'Silver Fox' Stephens, Maj Daniel Andre and Maj Noel Warner pose by the YF-12A that did the job: 60-6936. *Lockheed*

4 Lockheed's Georgia Division's 'Black' Birds

Also engaged in USAF Comint and Elint, battle area supervision, counter-C^3 and special forces support are a number of dedicated, modified C-130 Hercules. These, briefly, include the following:

Designation	Codename	Mission	Units and notes
AC-130A/H	Specter	Gunship armed with computer- and sensor-directed 20mm, 40mm and 105mm guns	16th SOS, 1st SOW, TAC, Hurlburt Field, Florida (10 AC-130H); and 711th SOS, 919th SOG, AFRES, Duke Field, Florida (10 AC-130A). The AC-130As are to be withdrawn in the early 1990s, to be replaced by 12 AC-130Us, under development
DC-130A/E/H	Combat Angel	Ryan RPV mothership	Operated with SAC's 350th SRS, 100th SRW at Bien Hoa, South Vietnam, then U-Tapao, Thailand, and later by TAC's 355th TFW and re-formed 432nd Tactical Drone Group at Davis-Monthan AFB, Arizona. Disbanded in 1979 and all 11 aircraft returned to the cargo configuration
EC-130E/H	Comfy Levi	Airborne Battlefield Command & Control Center (ABCCC), which co-ordinates friendly C^3	7th ACCS, 552nd AW&CW, TAC, Keesler AFB, Mississippi. Seven aircraft operational
EC-130E	Coronet Solo II	Battle area Comint	193rd ECS, 193rd ECG, ANG, Harrisburg, Pennsylvania (four Coronet Solo II Comint 'paddle' antenna and trailing wire EC-130E [RR], and four C^3 EC-130E[CL])
EC-130H	Compass Call	Battle area C^3/CM	41st ECS, TAC, Davis-Monthan AFB, Arizona; and 66th ECW, USAFE, Sembach AB, West Germany. Five aircraft each
MC-130E	Combat Talon	Special Forces infiltration machine	8th SOS, 1st SOW, TAC, Hurlburt Field, Florida, 7th SOS, USAFE, Rhein-Main, West Germany; and 1st SOS, PACAF, Clark Field, the Philippines. Fourteen MC-130Es operational; due to be supplemented by 24 new MC-130H Combat Talon IIs, under development